NEU-CO WINNING RELATIONSHIPS

RE-BUILD TRUST . EARN CREDIBILITY
Breakthrough collection of techniques to
manage emotions in personal & professional relationships

BINDU BHATIA

INDIA · SINGAPORE · MALAYSIA

Notion Press

Old No. 38, New No. 6
McNichols Road, Chetpet
Chennai - 600 031

First Published by Notion Press 2018
Copyright © Bindu Bhatia 2018
All Rights Reserved.

ISBN 978-1-64324-002-2

This book has been published with all reasonable efforts taken to make the material error-free after the consent of the author. No part of this book shall be used, reproduced in any manner whatsoever without written permission from the author, except in the case of brief quotations embodied in critical articles and reviews.

The Author of this book is solely responsible and liable for its content including but not limited to the views, representations, descriptions, statements, information, opinions and references ["Content"]. The Content of this book shall not constitute or be construed or deemed to reflect the opinion or expression of the Publisher or Editor. Neither the Publisher nor Editor endorse or approve the Content of this book or guarantee the reliability, accuracy or completeness of the Content published herein and do not make any representations or warranties of any kind, express or implied, including but not limited to the implied warranties of merchantability, fitness for a particular purpose. The Publisher and Editor shall not be liable whatsoever for any errors, omissions, whether such errors or omissions result from negligence, accident, or any other cause or claims for loss or damages of any kind, including without limitation, indirect or consequential loss or damage arising out of use, inability to use, or about the reliability, accuracy or sufficiency of the information contained in this book.

Contents

Preface — v
Acknowledgements — ix

1. Mind-Body Connection — 1
2. Change in "Me" — 9
3. Permission — 14
4. Re-Building Trust — 22
5. The Power of Belief — 28
6. Dealing with Difficult Relationships — 37
7. Happiness Redefined — 46
8. Managing Our Reactions — 53
9. Intentions: Did You Really Mean That? — 65
10. Managing Expectations — 70
11. Perceptions & Conflicts — 95
12. Love & Attachment — 103
13. The Depth of "Communication" — 111
14. Emotional Vocabulary — 118
15. Gratitude List — 124
16. Affirmations — 129
17. Winning Frames — 151
18. Empowering Beliefs for Winning Mindset — 157

Summing Up — 159
References — 161

Preface

How this book can bring abundance in your life?

This book is going to change your life, I know. What you are about to read has already changed mine and many other millions of people who have been following some or more of these tools.

Why to read this book?

It is very simple to understand, learn and practice.

All of us are well aware of what to do if we have physical issues like headache, a cut or burn etc. We have learnt this formally and informally too.

But do you really know exactly what to do if someone hurts us, back stabs us, is rude to us, or if people gang up on us, if we feel left out, or when we fail, are let down etc.

Unfortunately, in our education system, very little has been taught formally about emotional hurts, burns and aches.

Our reactions majorly rely on what we have seen, experienced and how we have translated this information in our brains. That's why different people follow different practices. It's a gray area – some reactions work some don't!

If you want to learn some tested winning formulas about how to manage your emotions, lead your dream life, attract abundance, and build long lasting relationships and rapport with people, then this book is the right choice for you.

If you want to re-set your life, re-program it to be more successful and happy specially when it comes to relationships at work and in life, then I can promise you that it takes nothing more than following a proven recipe, that is exactly what this book delivers.

This book is a culmination of all tools/techniques that I practiced and learnt over the last 20 years. Nothing that I speak about in this book is untested.

Preface

It can be a life changing process for you, if you are really committed. I will be truly humbled to know if this book impacted you and how.

If any of the following statement hold true for you -

1. There's something or the other that goes wrong most of the times in relationships
2. People are generally unhappy with you or you are generally unhappy with people
3. You can't trust people easily, or people don't tend to trust you
4. You are unable to make a genuine connect with others
5. You feel that you are not able to manage your emotions internally and externally

Inability to manage these emotions with people/relationships, go a long way to deteriorate not only your body/health, but also, your career, relationships and other happy factors in life.

This book is an effort from me, to share with you, few of my favorite tools/techniques that enabled me to win back my relationships, love people unconditionally and remain calm in the most stressful situations.

Even if you take away 1% of what is shared in the book and apply in your life, my purpose is met and I'm sure yours will too.

What is this book all about?

The book is divided into 3 sections:

1. The first part of the book is about creating a **Winning Mindset**. The aim is to understand the core concepts regarding our brain and how we operate in natural circumstances. Like any exercise or diet regime starts with a warm up or detoxification, chapters in this section cover some key aspects of human brain and thought processes, which have to be geared up, before we jump into the main aspect of the book i.e. relationships.
2. The second part of this book talks about building the **Winning Relationships**, and how we can nurture them, with simple daily tools &

techniques. It includes some breakthrough formulas to manage emotions, conflicts, forgiveness, decisions, prioritization and expectations in all kinds of relationships. Explained with numerous real-life and relatable stories and examples.

3. The third part of the book is a quick implementable set of ***Winning Habits to follow***, which are just like plug and play technology. Follow these extremely simple habits, and see your whole life changing in front of you. This section includes a ready list of 200+ winning beliefs, affirmations and rules to create your own set.

What will you take away?

There are some pathbreaking simple tools mentioned in the book, following which you will be able to -

1. Look at things objectively
2. Manage your emotions better to make long-lasting beautiful relationships at work and in personal life
3. Make better decisions using both logical and emotional aspects of mind
4. Prioritize your time and relationships better
5. Deal with internal fears and threats that might be stopping you today to achieve success and happiness

Over a period of time, you will also see your **overall health improving**. Manage those BP, depression, diabetes, thyroid and other mid-to-mild physical/mental disorders, that are a result of the emotional stress you've been carrying for months and years.

To take the best out of this book remember these 2 things

1. **Stay committed, stay focused and TRUST your mission to bring about a positive abundance in your life**
2. **Sometimes you might not agree or resonate with one tool or technique – remember "IT's OK" – move on to the new chapter new tool. Not everything resonates with everyone**

Preface

Bindu Bhatia

Life Coach & People development strategist

Founder – M/S NeuCode Talent Academy LLP

A Note from the Author

"As a man was passing the elephants, he suddenly stopped, confused by the fact that these huge creatures were being held by only a small rope tied to their front leg. No chains, no cages. It was obvious that the elephants could, at any-time, break away from their bonds but for some reason, they did not.

He saw a trainer nearby and asked why these animals just stood there and made no attempt to get away. "Well," trainer said, "when they are very young and much smaller we use the same size rope to tie them and, at that age, it's enough to hold them. As they grow up, they are conditioned to believe they cannot break away. They believe the rope can still hold them, so they never try to break free."

Dear reader,

Like the elephant in the story above, all of us also have some deep conditionings that hold us back from attaining the ultimate success, happiness and satisfaction in life. This book has the capability to not only elicit those unconscious conditionings, but also re-programming them, so that you can break your rope and tread faster and higher in life.

If you benefit from this book or if you have feedback to share, please feel free to write to me at bindu.bhatia@neucodetalent.com

I'm deeply humbled that you picked up this book and really hope it brings a positive difference in your life and relationships.

Happy reading,
Bindu Bhatia

Acknowledgements

For people who made a big difference in my life

Life brings a lot of challenges! What makes a difference is – "how we respond to them." We must have heard this phrase in thousand different ways.

I believe - "How we respond to these challenges" is also directly correlated to the kind of relationships we have with people around us.

"*Our guides, philosophers, mentors, relatives, friends, colleagues etc. all play a very important role in how we respond to challenges in lives.*"

Positive relationships bring "abundance," while negativity in relationships significantly bring down our happiness, success and abundance capacity.

Life has bestowed a lot of blessings on me, and without thanking them, I just can't move ahead with the book.

My two solid epitomes of positivity – my dad (Mr. R.K. Bharani) and my husband (Mr. Harish Bhatia). Thanks to both of them for making me stand, when I touched the rock bottom in life.

Mom (Mrs. Adesh Bharani) to teach me what unconditional love is, and how simplicity is still the world's most precious virtue to have.

My daughter **Inaayat**, who is my inspiration to write. I wish she grows up to build mature and winning relationships with people and shower more love and light in the world.

My in-laws Mrs. RajKumari Bhatia, Mr. Nanak Bhatia, without whose support I wouldn't have managed to live an abundant life that I am living today. I owe all of this - writing a book, managing my successful career, baby and home, to them.

Acknowledgements

My brother – Mohit Arora, who spent endless hours with me to get this final version of the book printed. Can't thank you enough for all the love & patience you bestow on me everytime we meet.

My friend Snehal Kamath(Mankikar), who took out time, read the manuscripts and gave so much more life to this book. Each time she wrote a searing feedback with an intention to make it the BEST, my heart was overwhelmed with gratefulness for existence of such friends in my life. Despite going through her own time and life challenges, taking time out for this purpose means a lot to me.

Some more people to thank who guided me relentlessly from my childhood to shape me how I am today as a person –

Mr. Kishi & Mrs. Manisha Malhotra, Mr. Davinder and Dr. Harinder Sandhu – All 4 of them are my guiding & protecting angels. This book is my effort to make a difference to other people's lives, the way they did in my life.

Shishir's parents, Dr. R.S. Verma & Mrs. Saroj Verma who despite losing their son, made a decision to get their widowed daughter in law re-married! If I have bounced back in my life, and am standing somewhere in my career, it's because both of them supported me, going against their society measures and rituals.

Last, but not the least, my spiritual guide – Mr. Suresh Kumar Mahabal, who played a key role in my journey to happy life and relationships.

01

Mind-Body Connection

The greatest revolution of our generation is the discovery that human beings, by changing the inner attitudes of their minds, can change the outer aspects of their lives.

— **William James, American psychologist**

Before diving deeper into the relationships and it's dynamics, it is important for us to be aware of some core concepts about our mind.

Concept 1: Reality & Imagination

After a lot of debate, we decided to watch Bajrangi Bhaijaan – a Bollywood movie with my favorite star – Salman Khan, the reviews were raving about the emotions and acting. I was excited. My husband is not a big Bollywood fan, so you can imagine his plight. Sitting next to me, he ordered a lot of food to pass his time. Lights went dim and the show started!

I was glued with the character shown by Salman and was amazed at the little girl's acting. Just before intermission, I suddenly heard some sobs besides me – argh! Whaaaat?? Are you crying??? – I asked my husband, with a surprise and a grin on my face.

He looked at me reluctantly and said – "I can't take emotions when it comes to children"… he pulled out from the chair and went to washroom. Luckily just then, intermission happened, he returned after some time and we had our bit of chuckles.

He had tears in his eyes. But why? It's just a movie not the reality.

There are more examples to understand this fundamental –

1. Thinking about cutting a fresh yellow/green lemon can make your mouth watery, sometimes you can even feel the sour taste.

2. Have you ever got tears thinking about some past memories? The moment is gone, it's not a present reality anymore, but by just reliving that memory you can experience those related emotions and body symptoms all over again. For example: If you are remembering a great experience, your body will start feeling the same excitement, energy and even sweat at times, similarly if you are remembering a bad moment, you might have the same feelings, throat filled, tears in the eyes, heaviness in breathing etc.

That's the truth of our brain. In summary -

> **"Our brain doesn't know the difference between reality and imagination."**

We provide the brain a stimulus through real life, memories or through media like movies, video games etc., and the brain starts ordering the body to release the related chemicals, and our body starts reacting – be it heaviness in throat, tears in eyes, pain in the body!

So, our body is just acting up based on the signals from the mind. Mind sends signals based on the stimulus it gets through any form of medium/senses.

In nutshell, whatever we tell our brain becomes true for it, and it starts working on the response/reactions.

Concept 2: Literal Meaning of the Words

My granny used to say – "Speak carefully, as sometimes god is sitting on your tongue and whatever you say will come true"

It's a common saying – but I understood what it means quite late in life. I started observing my coaching clients, friend and relatives.

Their problems and narration of challenges were so close to the physical issues they were facing in life.

One of my friends, was under a tremendous debt. She hadn't told anyone in the family about it. She use to tell me how much burden she feels on her back, and what all she has to do to hide it from her relatives. To my shock after a couple of months, she told me that she had a lower back pain and doctor diagnosed it as slip disc!

Another friend of mine had this habit of saying "Pain in the a**," after some time I heard, she frequently suffered from constipation and piles.

One coachee was explaining how she felt hurt and wounded from the betrayal from her own family members, and later I was told that she was suffering badly from ulcers in the stomach.

Another one, told me vividly how she was heart-broken and wanted some peace and ability to trust others in life. She had chronic BP issues.

Now – all of this and many more, cannot be a co-incidence. There are a lot of researches that have proven that our mind and body are connected. Whatever – GOOD or BAD you tell your mind, it impacts body!

Cough, allergies, cold, throat problems have been related to communication issues in life. i.e. you are likely to suffer with these symptoms, if you have a lot to say but are unable to say.

Stress is medically proven to be related to depression, BP, Thyroid etc.

So now, that you've understood how your mind and body is connected, there is one more evident take away -

> "Carefully choose the words that you use for self, others, situations etc. Mind always takes your words Literally"

Concept 3: Pre-Programming for a Stimulus Make Us React

There is yet another truth about our brain/mind which needs to be understood very clearly before we move ahead.

(PS. – I'm using the words brain and mind interchangeably here, while there are lot of debates and definitions about the subject)

This one day, I shouted and jumped back on the bed from the floor. Started screaming and was petrified to see this giant flying cockroach right in front of me. I froze and had no idea what to do next.

My house help came running, and saw the cockroach, she quickly took out her slipper and hit it hard, picked up with hand and went back smiling. I just laid back down on my bed to get back my breathing to normal. What would I do if I witnessed a snake or a lion? Argghh...

In some time, my logical brain started working and was making terrible fun of me. It was just a cockroach, what could it do? Why such a strong reflex?

Mind-Body Connection

Needless to say, it was the topic of discussion on the dining table that night. People had a good laugh on my expense. My husband being an ardent animal/insect lover, said "you scared the poor thing to death, he must be more scared than you!." As if this wasn't enough, he said "Have you ever noticed a cockroach, they are so cute with those two little antennas moving around." I still don't find it possible to find a cockroach CUTE.. but yes, the point is, there are 3 people in this scene thinking differently about a stimulus (cockroach in this case) -

- Me – I find a cockroach an ugly and creepy creature and am petrified if I witness anything like that.
- My Maid – For her, cockroach is just like another mosquito, she could casually just hit it, hold it with hand and throw away!
- My Husband – who finds a cockroach – CUTE and empathize with its' life.

Here's the answer that appealed to me the most -

It is not about what cockroaches really are, what they are capable or not capable of doing factually.

The fact here is that my brain has been programmed to fear a cockroach. Looking back – I remember my mom use to have the same reaction and I just mirrored it in my childhood.

Most of us in the urban population are terribly scared of snakes, however, what makes villagers so casual about them? It's the programming of brain.

Now, what's this programming that we are talking about here? Let me explain this in simple words in the next concept. It will answer a key question – why we react the way we do for some things/people?

If you are able to understand this next concept, it has the power to convert your reactions to a positive response immediately.

Concept 4: Triune Brain Theory & Programming

This concept answers some very important questions - Why we react the way we do? Why different people react differently in same situations?

Dr. Paul Maclean, a leading neuroscientist, developed the famous Triune Brain theory for understanding the brain in terms of its evolutionary history. According to this theory, three distinct brains emerged successively in the course of evolution and now co-inhabit the human skull.

1. **Neocortex**/new brain/logical brain
2. **Limbic system**/emotional brain
3. **Reptilian Brain**/survival instincts

These three parts of the brain do not operate independently. They have established numerous neuro pathways through which they influence one another.

Looking at each of these 3 parts, and how they interplay can be very interesting to understand our own reactions and responses.

I've seen major transformations in people just by knowing about this whole process.

Here's a very simple explanation about how all of them work together to decide our actions/reactions and responses to various stimulus.

Before we begin, it is important to always remember that

> "The key role of our brain is to protect us from danger. Our brain works on survival instinct all the time"

Now, let's look at the figure 1.0 closely and understand how it all works together.

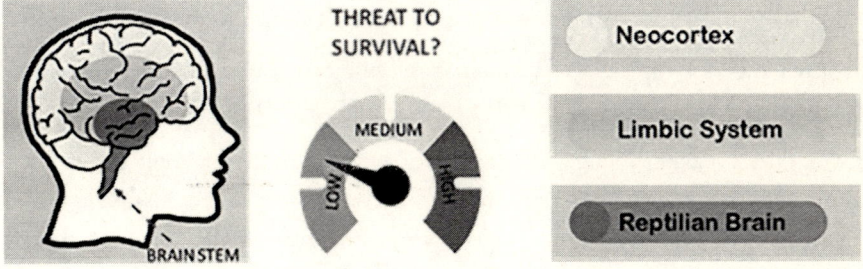

Figure 1.0 Triune Brain Theory

All of us are aware of the 5 senses (See, Hear, Touch, Taste and Smell). These senses are responsible to pick up information from the environment. Stimulus from the environment is passed on to the first brain – *Reptilian brain*.

For each stimulus that our brain attends, *threat level to survival* is calculated in fractions of a second. For ease of understanding, let's divide it into 3 levels – HIGH. MEDIUM. LOW.

Situation 1: If the stimulus is perceived to be HIGH threat information, **Reptilian brain** gets immediately active, releases energy from all possible sources, to put it all into the reaction to save us from the danger. Example: at the sight of a snake, we might not emote or think, we will only quickly react!

Situation 2: If the stimulus from the brain stem is perceived to be MEDIUM threat information, reptilian brain sends the information to limbic system, where the information is processed further, basis previous experiences and translations. Owing to the programming done earlier, related hormones are released which result in us feeling and reacting to those emotions.

Example: If we lose our wallet in a moving bus in an unknown city, the first possible reaction would be to feel shocked, increased palpitation etc. only after few seconds, when the information goes to the neo-cortex, will we take the logical decisions like blocking the cards, search for the wallet.

Information is not able to go further to neocortex (logical brain), till these chemicals/hormones settle down. That's why at times

Situation 3: If the stimulus is perceived to be LOW threat information, then it seamlessly passes it on to the neo-cortex for logical thinking. That's why we are able to have a point of view and solutions for general or third-party information, like buying a house, what to cook today, which restaurant to go for dinner etc.

Now that we understand that our reactions to a stimulus depends on "Threat level" that we have assigned to it, let's look at how we create these threat perceptions.

This calculation of threat level happens basis our own previous experiences and translations in life.

For example, a person living in a rural area might not have a high threat level programming for a non-poisonous snake, however for urban population a snake irrespective of its breed, is highly dangerous, even the sight of the snake can trigger extreme reaction.

These threat levels are assigned by us since childhood and are stored in our subconscious memories. That's why, in some cases we don't even remember why we react to certain situations, the way we do.

Let me give you an example, when I was very young, my mom often used to say – "Don't ever trust people with light color eyes!" Just a statement without any facts and data. I took it as a threat level medium-high. Now until recently, I realized that most of the people who I got into conflicts with, or I avoided, rejected for no obvious reasons, had one thing in common – "LIGHT EYES." A big revelation to me, once I understood the reason, I re-programmed myself by telling my brain -it's ok, everyone is trust-worthy, that information was not based on facts, so I can ignore.

Similarly, wild animals are dangerous. The threat level is programmed as HIGH and we are naturally going to react almost similarly when we encounter wild animals.

So, the next fact about our brain is that

> **"Brain responds to a stimulus based on the Threat level that we have associated with it"**

For example, in today's world, we don't encounter wild animal that frequently, but we do encounter situations similar to these, that most likely we have placed in high threat zone–

- Our boss calls us to ask for a surprise presentation to very senior leadership
- We need to present data to clients and that's the making or breaking point of the deal
- We have a high-profile presentation to more than 1000 people from the industry or so on…

The threats have changed, however, our mind/body's response to these threats remains the same. We still feel the pressure, tingling feeling, nervousness, shaking legs, butterflies in the tummy etc.

If we can re-programme these threat levels for some selective stimuli which are dis-empowering us, we can easily change our reaction to it.

In the following chapters, you will learn many tools to make it happen. Be open and reflective while reading.

Summary | Chapter 1

Before we move ahead, here are 3 facts about brain/mind that we must remember –

- Our brain doesn't know the difference between **reality and imagination**.
- Carefully choose the words that you use for self, others, situations etc. **Mind** always takes stimulus (the words) **Literally.**
- **Brain responds** to a stimulus based on **"threat level"** we have associated with it.

Reader Reflections

1. How much do you rate yourself (from 1 to 10, 1 being the lowest), when it comes to your immediate overall relationships–

   a. At Work

   b. In Personal Life

2. List down the names of people you'd like to mend your relationship with.

3. Are there any specific situations, where you always react without thinking through and regret later? List down the deep-down threat levels that are attached to these situations.

   In subsequent chapters, we will learn how to deal with these fears and threats.

02

Change in "Me"

Why those self-change promises don't work most of the times?

Is Change a Pain or a Pleasure for You?

This is quite a recent revelation for me too. I always thought that any kind of change that I want to bring in myself will initially come with a lot of pain. But that's a myth.

The fact is, if you are feeling a disturbing pain (physical or emotional) to change yourself, then you are not following the right process and most likely you will come back to the status quo in some time. One needs to feel eustress when making changes in self, instead of de-stress. Let me explain the concept of eustress and destress before we move ahead –

Eustress – is the positive stress. For example – you love your dance class, after a tiring day at work, you have a session, when you go there and find your favorite music playing, you gather some energy and dance your heart out. Once you are back home in the night, you are tired, but excited, satisfied, proud and happy too… that's EUSTRESS.

Destress – on the other hand is negative stress. For example – Yet another tiring day at work, a job that you find mundane. The moment you are about to leave, your boss calls you and requests you to do 2 more hours of work, it's an urgent client escalation. Most likely you will feel extremely tired, stressed out, and drained once you come back. That's Destress.

To attain Eustress out of any change that you want to make in your life, you need to have **right positive reasons**, and a clear answer for yourself as to WHY you want that change? What will it get you? If you love the reason, and really want it, the change won't stress you that much.

*The question you need to ask yourself is – do you **really** want that change?*

My friend who really wanted to lose weight from a long time (few years), found every reason as to why she couldn't exercise. She said she had weak ligaments issue, arthritis, weight problem, so exercising is not the solution for her. Every 6 months I'd see an announcement from her on Facebook or other common platforms, but after few days things fizzled out. She was getting more and more disgusted by herself, her self-esteem had touched the rock bottom. She used to blame her weight for not getting any marriage alliance.

One day I used a provocative coaching technique and blasted her! I told her if "Weight" is such a big disastrous issue in your life then better leave everything else and you just FOCUS on it like a maniac till it gets out of your way. She must have been a little surprised with my tone, but I was serious.

Next, I heard, she quit her organization, and decided to give herself a break before finding a new job. She searched for a great trainer, and within just 3 months, not only me, but her fitness trainer was himself surprised with the results.

The girl who complained about ligaments, arthritis and all kinds of issues, a girl who was advised by the doctors to not do heavy exercise, the one who use to feel terrible pain after only a brisk walk, was now a plank queen, her record was 11 minutes!!

Her workouts had become inspiration for many at the gym, she started advising people on their regimes, and needless to say she lost around 15kgs in 6 months.

In between she was telling me, how she had been trying to quit having tea for ages now, but it took her just that ONE minute to quit it forever!

I was myself inspired and surprised with her results.

The point I'm trying to make here is that making a change in your life should not bring you chronic pain (emotionally or physically).

> "Change process must give you more pleasure than pain, for it to be permanent"

How Do You Make Any Change a 'Pleasure?'

The key to make the change positive, is to have the RIGHT reasons within self, to change that part of your life.

I have also fallen prey to this game of "losing weight" and always fell flat, and later realized that I never ever really wanted it so bad. I wanted to be fit, and look good, and I managed to do that even with some extra pounds in my body. As long as I'm fit, my medical reports are fine, I have all the energy to do my chores I'm happy with myself.

When you **really want** to bring a change in your life, it will happen very naturally and most of the times it is a pleasure.

In my leadership development workshops, I stress on this fact. If you as a leader want to bring some positive change in the organization which is impacting employees, then it has to be translated in a way that employees see their own benefit in that change. Any failure to build "What's in it for employees" will make all these change efforts worthless and create a negative environment.

This can also be explained in terms of "Purpose." The current generation is excited and gives its best output when they know "Why" they are doing something. A very apt example I heard in one of the videos was – A leader walked up to a janitor in NASA and asked what are you doing? Janitor's response was – Sir, I'm helping a man go to the moon.

A famous story explains it even more beautifully,

"A man came across three masons who were working at chipping chunks of granite from large blocks. The first seemed unhappy at his job, chipping away and frequently looking at his watch. When the man asked what it was that he was doing, the first mason responded, rather curtly, "I'm hammering this stupid rock, and I can't wait 'til 5 when I can go home."

"A second mason, seemingly more interested in his work, was hammering diligently and when asked what it was that he was doing, answered, "Well, I'm molding this block of rock so that it can be used with others to construct a wall. It's not bad work, but I'll sure be glad when it's done."

"A third mason was hammering at his block fervently, taking time to stand back and admire his work. He chipped off small pieces until he was satisfied that it was the best he could do. When he was questioned about his work he stopped, gazed skyward and proudly proclaimed, "I…am building a cathedral!"

"Three men, three different attitudes, all doing the same job."

So, remember another fact about change.

Change for a "larger purpose" will not only come easily, without pain, but also bring loads of pleasure and happiness.

Why we are talking about this topic is, because, time and again while reading this book you need to keep giving your brain the reasons, what will you get by implementing your knowledge gained from this book. The change is not threatening, it instead will bring you more pleasure and abundance in life, provided you have the RIGHT reasons to change.

Summary | Chapter 2

- **Positive changes** in life give you **more pleasure** than pain
- Change for a **"larger purpose"** will not only come easily, without pain, but also will bring loads of pleasure and happiness

P.S.: There are times when change that comes to your life is not voluntary, it just hits you hard leaving you with no choice. Dealing with those situations is a very different task altogether. We will be covering that aspect later in the book.

Reader Reflections

1. Select an area where you want to experience change or a different result
2. List actions that you can take towards this change
3. Write about the pain of not taking the action towards the results
4. Write about how it will feel like to achieve your goal
5. Notice the motivation that you can generate by flipping the pain and pleasure
6. What is clear to you now?

03

Permission

Permit yourself to be deeply "OK" with situations and people.

This is by far the most important self-management tool one can imbibe. Not only you will grow as a person, but also as a coach, as a counselor, as a friend and in any other relationship. It might take some time to program yourself, but once done, most of your challenges will be resolved by themselves.

Permission to Let Go of the Negative Emotions Attached to "Situations"

At 24yrs of age, I lost my first husband to god. The whole life and soul shattered right in front of me. I bottled up myself with emotions and blamed myself for so long that it became impossible for me to even smile. I was certainly not ok with the situation.

I remember after around 6 months of the incident, one day, I went to watch a movie with my mom, and we found it very weird and stupid, so stupid that the moment we came out of the hall perplexed and confused to react, we laughed out loud.

Suddenly, I realized that I laughed for the first time after the incident. Immediately, at the same moment while I was laughing, tears filled my eyes and I started crying out even louder.

That day I realized, that I was carrying the guilt and was not permitting myself to be happy again!

That was the turning point, and it still took me a lot of time to get out of that guilt and feel normal. I wish I knew these tools earlier.

To explain this better, let me share few more examples of my coaching clients -

"A student, who went through sexual abuse when she was just 5-year old, carried the guilt and shame till date (she's 22yr old now), and felt that she cannot have any relationship. She had not permitted herself to get into any relationship owing to the guilt and shame of the incident that happened 15+ years ago!"

"A 39-year old employee who reached only an assistant manager level in an organization, despite giving last 11 years to it, told me that he was somehow not able to ask for hikes and promotions. He used to feel extremely embarrassed and demeaned to ask for it. Upon reflecting more, he realized he wasn't internally permitting himself to grow, because in his mind growth in career will mean compromising on the family time. The moment he realized this, he reprogrammed and clarified his brain, reduced the threat level and now he has started his own company with ~50lakh turnover already."

I was coaching "a mid-age homemaker, who took a decision to take care of kids instead of making her own career. She was extremely blessed to have abundance in life from any normal person's point of view. However, she opted for a coaching session with me, because she was feeling very incomplete in life, she felt something big is missing in her life. Her daily chores had choked her so much that she started taking out her frustration on kids and husband.

After some reflection, she realized that she had the guilt of "being at home" and the fact she is not contributing enough in terms of finances, she never permitted herself to enjoy life, go out for lavish vacation, shopping or do something for herself. The moment she re-programmed herself and consciously gave herself all the credit and permissions, she's enjoying life to the fullest now. I keep watching her Facebook updates and feel happy."

In all the cases above, the one thing that is common is – **Guilt and Permission.**

The fact is that sometimes there is a guilt, or experiences which prevent us to enjoy the freedom. *Even if no one is stopping, we feel the pressure in our own heads.*

I belonged to a lower middle-class family, I don't remember going to any shop and buy stuff for myself, it was always from the streets and stalls. After years, even when

Permission

I started earning lakhs in a month, it took me so many years to go to branded stores and buy stuff for myself. I wasn't able to permit myself to give in to that abundance!

Free yourself from the guilt and permit yourself to enjoy and absorb the happiness & abundance that has been blessed on you.

Note: Of course. you take a calculated decision about how much you can splurge, how much can your eco-system absorb, but starving for happiness and abundance is not fair. Listen to yourself and know when to stop. Balance is important.

Re-programming to "BE OK" with situations

- **Identify** – What is it that you really want to do, but just can't.
- **Clarify** – Will this action bring you more peace, happiness and maintain the balance in your ecosystem (Family, finances etc.)?
- **Affirmations** - Repeat these at-least 10–20 times a day till these become your reality.
    - ✓ I deserve all the happiness in life
    - ✓ I choose to let go all the feelings and thoughts that were stopping me so far
    - ✓ I set myself free from here on
    - ✓ I deserve to lead a happy and abundant life
    - ✓ I permit myself to enjoy my life and go for stuff I have always wanted to go for
    - ✓ I welcome peace, trust, acceptance, and safety into my life

To sum up this concept, if some situation in the past is holding you back, if it is refraining you from moving towards happiness, abundance and balance, then all you need to do is give "Permission" to yourself using affirmation or language part of the brain.

> *"Remember our brain needs that permission verbally, that's why repeating these affirmations do wonders. Brain only take stimulus – it doesn't bother whether it's a reality or imagination. It just believes what you tell it. So, tell the right things to brain and it will work the right way!"*

Permission to Let Go of Negative Emotions Attached to "People"

One of my coachee, who is a well-qualified and fairly successful businesswoman came to me with a very heavy heart.

She said, you might find it bizarre, but here's a problem that I'm dealing with. Despite a lot of efforts I'm unable to find peace with my in-laws. The way they treated me and made me feel in the early years of my marriage is just unforgivable. Even today, I just feel that heaviness when there is any mention of them or when some topic about my marriage comes up. This upsets my husband and we get into a fight or an argument.

What was more surprising for me was, when she told me – "The problem is that I can't even patch up or take out my frustration or vent out, because they are not alive." They passed away around 5 years ago.

Now this one was tricky!

Similarly, I remember it took me just few seconds to feel the anger all over my body, whenever I thought of this relative of mine. She used to leave no chance to humiliate me in every possible way in every possible meeting. Years and years passed by, I just could never neutralize my feelings, and no matter how old and successful I became, her mention would just burn me up from within! And yes, I suffered from burning sensation in my chest due to gas, a lot during all those days and years 😉

I'm sure you can relate these feelings with "that" someone in your life. The problem is that, these feelings, if not taken care of, can cause big diseases as well. Because all said and done we have buried those ill-feelings in our sub-conscious, and we release toxins whenever these people are talked about, worse when we face these people in social settings or personally.

Tools to Forgive Others

Tool 1: "Seek permission" from within yourself, do you **really** want to let these feelings go?

Tool 2: If the answer is "NO," I can't forgive, then let's first clarify *what is FORGIVENESS*?

Forgiveness doesn't mean	Forgiveness means
Doing a favor to that person	Doing favor to myself, my equilibrium, increasing my own success potential

Permission

Forgiveness doesn't mean	Forgiveness means
Resuming the same relationship with that person	Choosing a better way to deal with that person, so he/she doesn't impact me anymore
Again getting emotionally connected to the person	Consciously choosing the way forward relationship with this person, to refrain yourself from getting hurt again
You are condoning the wrong or acting as if the person never hurt you	You are simply letting it go, for your own peace

Forgive quickly: Worse is - the more time you take to forgive someone or let go, the more difficult it will get, as your brain will keep that information permanently as a potential threat information, your brain will be programmed to react a certain way on the mention of this person or on seeing/meeting this person.

Tool 3: Now if you are not able to give permission to forgive this person. Keep arguing with yourself. Sometimes, brain loves the "VICTIM" feeling, check if you are getting some thrill out of becoming a victim.

Tool 4: Re-Program your brain using the following affirmations, to let go of your negative emotions attached to this person

- Everyone make mistakes including me, I choose to forgive and be the bigger one
- Bad events are like the river flowing in one direction, once gone flowing water in the river never comes back
- I permit myself to let go of all the negative emotions
- I choose to see good things in every situation and person
- The intent behind every action of all people is good for themselves
- All of us are imperfect
- I love people unconditionally, it doesn't matter what you've done to me, I still love you. I might not be the same with you, I might make some adjustments in my relationship with you, but I still love you
- Everyone is good at heart, circumstances at times are bad
- All bad experiences happen to us for a reason, to make us learn something, I learnt my lesson and choose to move on
- No negative event or emotion is worth my time, that can be used for attracting abundance instead. I choose to set myself free and embrace myself in all positivity around

- Everyone makes a choice that is best available to him/her, in difficult situations

Tool 5: Reflect on the following questions:

1. What are the top 2 learnings that you take for yourself from this whole relationship or situation?
2. Will this learning help you react better next time when this person/situation is mentioned or encountered?
3. Is this learning worth sharing with anyone going through a similar challenge?

Tool 6: Ask the following questions:

1. How is this negative feeling helping you?
2. How is this negative feeling against this person, creating a negative impact?
3. What does forgiving this person really mean to you?

Tool 7: Tell them how you feel

Last but the ***most impactful tool*** that never goes wrong, given that you still have access to that person.

- **Tell the person exactly the emotion that you felt, when he/she did _____**

Example: My eldest sister use to be very rude to me in childhood days, I never liked her and avoided her as much as I could. For years, even after we grew up, got married, the feeling wasn't that great. Internally, I always missed talking to her or having a warm relationship with her. I always felt bad about the way she treated me back then in childhood. Then came the day, when we had our first heartfelt talk and I told her –

"I use to feel very humiliated and hurt when you spoke to me rudely or made fun of me, in front of all relatives and whenever you commented on my borrowed clothes."

She was shocked to hear that. She didn't know how to react! She said – *"I never realized I did that to you. I was always very protective of you and hated the fact that you were getting influenced by others and were going on the wrong path!"*

Now that shocked me because I never thought that she even cared about me!

Here's the catch. Let's revisit what I told her initially –

Instead of saying *"I use to feel very humiliated and hurt......"*

if I had told her *"You were very bossy and aggressive back then, you treated me like a junk!"* – what do you think her reaction could be?

Permission

There is a subtle difference in these two statements. In statement 1, we are telling them how we felt! We are not attacking, judging or making an allegation on the other person.

This tool worked best for me, but yes, it needs –

- Practice – start with smaller confessions and then go for big ones 😊
- Exposing a bit of our vulnerable side (which means keeping ego at the backseat)

Possible reactions of people when you confess your feelings about their actions:

1. **They can get angry**: "What do you mean? I hurt you so much? I never made you feel comfortable? Are you blaming me?

    Keep your calm and say "I am just telling you my feeling, not expecting that you change, not asking for any explanations, but just want to let you know that I feel this way when you do or say this to me." It's up-to you what you do next time!"

2. **They can break down**, be sarcastic, or be surprised, or walk away, or even counter attack you

    a. Just be calm, composed and confident – there's nothing wrong in telling someone how you feel about their behavior, it's their time to deal with emotions, they will definitely come back with an explanation or apology. Be careful if they are heart patients or too old to take heavy emotions. Choose the right time and mood to have this conversation.

I'm sure some or the other tool above, will surely help you get some answers and make you feel at ease.

Summary | Chapter 3

1. To move on from negative situations and people, it is very important to give yourself the permission to be "OK" with what happened.

2. *Forgiveness is the key, some tools to forgive others.*

    a. Reflect on your learnings from the situation or events

    b. Avoid enjoying the VICTIM feeling and bounce back with self-esteem

    c. Command your brain to forgive and let go, using affirmations

    d. Tell them about how you feel about the situation or behavior – this works 99% of times; just needs some ego shedding from your side

3. In the end, remember there are some relationships that have nothing left in them, they drain you out completely. Choose carefully what you want to do. Dissociating is the best way-out in many cases. It hurts initially, but very beneficial in the long run.

Readers Reflections

- Think about one person or situation that keeps bothering you offline as well
- Now, use one of the tools in chapter 3 to "Let go"
- If you are up-to it, choose to go with this super cool tool to feel the magic -
    - ✓ Take a print of the lyrics of the song "LET IT GO" (Movie: Frozen)
    - ✓ Put up the song on high volume, start singing with it as loud as you can
    - ✓ Now dance to it's tune
    - ✓ While dancing, think about this person or situation
    - ✓ Do this for at-least 5 minutes and observe your feelings

04

Re-Building Trust

Are you leading a team that doesn't trust or listen to you enough? Have you just started managing a group of peers who are resisting your leadership?

Or, do you have some personal relationships where due to circumstances or your own challenge, the trust was lost?

Building trust with a new unknown group is relatively easier than RE-BUILDING trust with the existing group of people you are working with or you have relationship with.

Often new roles, new positions, or new learning, brings an awareness, that one needs a change in self-brand or style of working.

However, because of the existing **perceptions, baggage and grudges**, it becomes even more painful to change and **re-build trust**.

The process takes a bit of time, but there's nothing more gratifying than re-building trust in relationships. You gain much more than you lose in this process.

This chapter is for you to understand and work on the **3 steps** that can help you re-build that trust and equation in all kinds of relationships.

Step 1: Internal Dialogue

Carefully listen to your own internal dialogue when you are with these people. What do you say to yourself in your mind?

One eye opening experience of mine regarding internal dialogue was that -

> "Internal dialogue is not at all related to how close you are to that person or team!"

Internal dialogue is instead a quick processing by the brain, related to a situation or a person, you might not truly mean it. However, the fact is that it impacts your ***Reaction****."*

Brain is in an auto-pilot mode and keeps processing these dialogues. Most of the times we even ignore this process happening inside us.

Let me take an example to explain this better.

A team member (Sahil) who works closely with the manager (John), one day in a team meeting tells John - *"But John, how could you take the decision of changing shift-timings without consulting us?"*

John was taken aback and here's a quick view to his **Internal dialogue** -

- Who are you to question me? I am your boss, I have some rights.
- Hellooo.. what kind of tone that is? You are putting me into a spot!
- What the hell, will see you later.

Immediately after this inner dialogue - What do you think John's possible reaction will be?

He clinched and had a visible frown on his face, he looked disappointed, took a sip of water, and consciously put together his words and said - "There are times, when management needs to decide certain things, keeping all dimensions in mind. I expect all of you to follow these new guidelines from next week onwards"

Yes, irritation was seen on John's face, he was able to use politically correct words, but everyone could gauge that he was upset about it. As a result, team lost the trust on sharing their opinions with their manager John. Despite the fact, that John gave a politically correct answer, there was a long-lasting deficit in trust with his team.

In a lot of my sessions, people ask me - how can we prevent ourselves from reacting to situations that we regret later. Here's the answer - Be conscious about what is your inner dialogue at that time?

> **"Your internal dialogue is directly proportional to your reaction/response"**

Take the same example ahead, if John could have revised his inner dialogue to the following -

Re-Building Trust

1. My team expects a lot out of me.
2. I'm glad they are open enough to have such a dialogue with me, instead of gossiping behind me.
3. It's not about me, it's about the new decision that they are upset with.
4. Any change, brings about a fear in people, let me handle it carefully to ensure they understand how it will help them.

What do you think John's reaction/response will be?

It's only in the ***difficult situations***, when TRUST is assessed and built. It has nothing to do with your relationship with those people at other times.

Your micro reactions in those difficult moments impact trust and relationships, hence, the first step is to take care of the **"Inner dialogue"** that is being processed in the brain. It can be easily re-phrased next time when you are in that situation.

Step 2: Behavior

A behavior is defined by what one can "SEE" or "Videotape." There are a lot of do's and don'ts about behaviors that we have been listening, reading and learning about. There are some contradictions as well around the RIGHT behaviors for a manager/leader.

Years ago, for me to get work done from others, use to take a little longer than what was expected from my GO GETTER boss.

She was awesome and decided to coach me on this aspect. Her intention was to refrain/stop me to waste time in bringing collaboration and creating WIIFT(What's in it for them).

> ***She advised me to use the "F" word, she made me practice it too a couple of times.... I was never comfortable and gave up!***

While her intention was right, but swearing just didn't come to me naturally, so I decided to bear some loss associated with it. I changed my own approach and was a little more assertive and it worked well.

Later, with a lot of introspection here's what I learnt around leadership behavior and how I can decide myself which ones to imbibe.

I'm sure you know "Behaviors build our brands," now what if we reverse it -

> **"Define our brand to decide our behaviors"**

This exercise eased a lot of my queries, dilemmas around leadership behaviors.

One leader is happy using "F" word, as it gives her an internal power, and she wants to build the *"Fearless and Bold"* brand for her, while for me - the brand I want to build is *"Compassionate, Simple and Authentic"* - the F word doesn't go with it!

So, I started consciously choosing behaviors that go well with my aspired BRAND.

This is not as simple as it looks, let's ponder on this example -

In one of my sessions, there was a participant, who came late, sat behind the class and intermittently kept working on his laptop. I observed for half an hour and started the topic of brand as a leader.

Later he said - I want people to see me as a hard-worker, focused, and the one who can multi-task. He was very surprised to know that with his initial behavior in the class (coming late, working on laptop etc.), his brand was being perceived as - careless, messed up with time, indecisive of his priorities.

Hence, few important things to remember -

1. Ensure congruence between your aspired brand and behaviors by taking feedback as well as observing reactions of people who matter
2. There will always be some people who will disagree with your behavior, but is it making the desired impact on the ones' you want to re-build trust with? - that's what matters
3. Whenever in doubt what to say, just take few seconds to revive your brand image in mind and then decide your response.

Behavior is the key to build trust, therefore, carefully choose the brand you wish to build in different relationships and reflect on associated behaviors that match the brand you would like to build.

Step 3: Consistency

This is one big thing that I learnt from my boss & mentor, a long time ago - Deepak Patil.

Re-Building Trust

I still remember sitting in that cafeteria having lunch, he was coaching me on how to be consultative with the team members and not push things through my way.

During the conversation, I did realize that I had started pushing my team often and yes, I had burnt bridges with some of them.

I had this fear and asked him - now that they have already faced this brunt with me and they have a perceptions - what do I do, how do I remove that baggage and rough edges?

His words were - Bindu - **"CONSISTENCY"** is the key. They will distrust you when you start this new consultative approach, let them, it's normal. However,

> *"If you are consistent over a period of time with your new approach and behavior, they will eventually believe and trust you. They might even respect you more to bring about that change in yourself."*

Yes - I did it, and it worked like a magic! That's the best team that I've worked with so far in my career, and we are still glued together despite being in different organizations.

Later I implemented this learning, with a lot of people I had burnt my bridges, due to some or the other reasons, and it all started falling in place, as this time I was consistent with my new behavior.

The question is "HOW" or "WHY" does it work?

Think about our belief about "Sun Rises from the East." How is it a belief? It's a belief because it's associated with what we witness every-time, every day. Sun is **consistent** and rises from the east! It's a fact that we witness each day, and nobody can change this fact.

> *"A consistent behavior becomes a factual data for other people's brain, and the brain eventually accepts it after evaluating it for some time, and eventually this consistency re-builds the trust in relationships."*

Once you identify the behaviors you'd like to change towards others, that are coherent to your brand, the only best way to work on it and re-build trustworthy relationships is to be "consistent."

Summary | Chapter 4

1. Difficult situations are the ones where TRUST is assessed and built. It has nothing to do with your relationship with those people at other times. Your small reactions in those difficult moments impact trust and relationships, hence, the first step is to take care of the **"Inner dialogue"** that is being processed in the brain.

2. Behavior is the key to build trust, therefore, carefully choose the brand you wish to build in different relationships, and reflect on associated behaviors that match the brand you would like to build.

3. Once you identify the behaviors you'd like to change towards others, that are coherent to your brand, the only best way to work on it and re-build trustworthy relationships is to be "consistent."

@ *NCTA Copyright tool* **C.B.I.**

Consistency + **B**rand & behavior + **I**nner Dialogue = **Rebuilding trust**

Reader Reflections

- Think about a situation that triggers your reaction every-time! What do you tell yourself? What can you tell yourself instead next time when it happens?

    Now re-program your brain in advance for that situation and observe the results. *Write with pen on a paper – Next time when I get into this situation I will…….*

- Choose the brand that you want to build as a leader or in any relationship. Write down the behaviors that you will display, especially in tricky situations.

05

The Power of Belief

Is your belief system limiting you or empowering you?
"Beliefs have the power to create and the power to destroy."

– **Anthony Robbins**

Sometimes, even if you have all the skills, resources and plan in place, things go wrong! There are phases in life, when this happens, not once, not twice, but almost every freaking time you try.. Have you experienced it? If yes, then you must know this –

"One of the biggest reasons we don't achieve our goals & wishes, that too repeatedly, is because of our own embedded limiting beliefs"

This chapter covers some extremely important aspects of our belief system, which if unlocked, can create an abundant life that you wouldn't have even thought of.

Fundamental Facts about Beliefs

What is a Belief?

It's a feeling of certainty about what something means. For example: Success is an outcome of hard work, Time is money, Marriage is a huge responsibility etc.

Where do these beliefs come from?

Most of our beliefs are generalizations about our past, based on our interpretations of painful and pleasurable experiences.

These beliefs could have been created "Consciously or unconsciously." Sometimes it's the education of our parents, sometimes our interpretation of a situation. We may have beliefs about rights, duties, abilities, permissions and so on.

Types of beliefs:

Beliefs can be classified basis how they impact you. There are ***few beliefs that make you feel stressed, heavy and sad***. On the other hand, ***there are few that give you strength to move on or bounce back***.

For me following beliefs really helped in life –

- I'm a strong resilient woman
- I take challenges as an opportunity to shine more
- Give your 100% in whatever you do, else don't do

However, few that were counterproductive for me were –

- Money never comes easily, you need to work extremely hard for it!
- Life is tough and full of tests and challenges
- If I'm laughing, I'll have to cry harder in few days

Impact of Beliefs on Our Life

The more we think about our beliefs, the more it gets engraved in us. We tag things right and wrong and make important decisions of life, using our belief system.

Our behaviors and actions naturally start aligning to those beliefs and we define our self-identity with these beliefs. So much so, that *sometimes these beliefs start limiting us and sometimes these beliefs take us to a highest point in life.*

Common examples of limiting beliefs are given below:

- Life is tough and full of challenges
- If one tells the truth on face, relationships get sour
- If I get too close to people, I get hurt
- I never get what I badly want
- World is full of unsafe people, I shouldn't trust others
- My health won't allow me to pursue my dreams
- True love doesn't exist anymore

The Power of Belief

If you identify with any of the above beliefs and feel stuck in life, you are the chosen one who's meant to be reading this chapter.

Tools to Work on "Limiting Beliefs"

1. Validate if it is really a "Limiting Belief"

   There is a question of whether limiting beliefs are actually good for us and whether they keep us away from any harm. In practice some beliefs which limit us are actually *valid beliefs* which are worth keeping. The problem is telling the difference.

   Limiting beliefs are erroneous, are based on wrong 'facts' and they prompt us to treat things with undue caution. Example: *You should never trust anyone in business.*

2. Question your limiting beliefs.

   The moment we begin to honestly question our beliefs and the experiences we assign to them, we no longer feel absolutely certain about them.

   Questions like these really help:

   - ✓ According to whom?
   - ✓ For whom?
   - ✓ What makes me think so?
   - ✓ What are the facts behind this?
   - ✓ Are there other people who have a different belief than this?
   - ✓ Could it be untrue?
   - ✓ Is this still applicable?

   This opens the door to replacing your old, dis-empowering beliefs with new beliefs that support you in the direction you want to go.

   Let me explain this with an example

   "I was in a coaching session with a director of a company, who was sharing how he was so naturally open to folks in his local team, peers, and colleagues in office, however, his growth was getting delayed because of lack of connect with global stakeholders. His 360 survey also revealed the same thing.

He said –"It's natural for me to ask you how'z your daughter doing and start a conversation, but I just cannot ask the same question from a global counterpart, even if he/she is initiating a small talk on a personal front."

He said he gets very anxious and it all feels at a very surface level. He was deeply upset about it and wondered what the reason could be.

After some time during the session, while he was recalling some portions of his childhood, he said, my dad always use to say - "This is our family, and we should never talk about personal things outside these four walls, and never let anyone come in between us."

I could see him getting uncomfortable and going deeper into reflection... after few minutes of silence he had an AHA moment and said – "Yes bindu I got it! In my map of the world, I was considering this belief to be true for my local workplace as my family and global counterparts as outsiders."

He couldn't believe, how relieved he was feeling, he got his answer and went back happy. He got promoted within next 6 months - and he wrote to me a note of thanks to make him aware of his biggest "Limiting Belief."

3. Replace your limiting belief with one or more empowering belief(s)

For example: When I started freelance coaching, it was very difficult for me to ask for a fee. I was ok providing services at lower rates or even free, than to negotiate or influence the client for what I deserved.

Later I realized that this was owing to my following limiting beliefs:

- ✓ If I charge or negotiate, people will doubt my intention to make a difference in their lives
- ✓ Money discussions are dangerous, they only bring more conflicts in relationships

Without any delays, I started questioning these beliefs and found that these are baseless translations that I had made in my childhood looking at some people fighting over money. Now I do charge for my services gracefully, and truly believe that.

- ✓ I deserve to be paid for the quality of my services
- ✓ Money discussions and contracting is actually important to iron-out any future conflict.

Once you have identified your limiting beliefs, it is very simple to replace them with some really powerful empowering beliefs. Remember, it doesn't matter if you doubt those empowering beliefs initially, over a period if you continue to tell your brain something, it will accept.

Remember, our brain literally accepts things that we tell it. So, the sooner you start telling your brain some powerful empowering beliefs, it will start accepting more abundance.

Here are few examples of empowering beliefs, feel free to create your own as well -

a. I am a power house! I attract success in everything I do

b. I always have time to do stuff that I really want

c. The past does not equal the future

d. Everything happens for good, we might not know the reason at the time it is happening, but there is always one good reason for what we are going through

e. I find great joy in little things... a smile... a flower... a sunrise...

f. I love freely because it is part of being human

g. Come what may, I have the power to bounce back

h. I get the best that I deserve, and if I don't get it, its for my own good

i. Any challenge in life only inspires me to do more and more

j. A great & transparent communication in any relationship

k. There is a goodness and core innocence in all human beings, exploring that space is beautiful

l. I respect all point of views and disagreements

m. I believe in taking immediate actions after the planning is done

4. Energize and empower your beliefs each morning.

   a. Write your empowering beliefs somewhere and read every morning. *By doing this you strengthen your neural pathways and finally it becomes permanent belief in 21 days of daily repeat.*

   b. Think about all the times when you were able to change any of your belief in the past, example – you believed that you could never drive a car, but you learnt and can drive now

> "Every action that we take, every decision that we make, every success that we get and every failure that we face – is an outcome of this powerful system within us called – BELIEF"

The danger of the BELIEF SYSTEM is that, if left unidentified, limiting beliefs can end you up into repeated failures with an unknown reason, deteriorates health - as it causes anxiety and lower self-esteem, refrains you from getting success that you really want.

The beauty of the BELIEF SYSTEM is that, the moment you identify the limiting beliefs, you can question it's integrity, confirm it's authenticity and can easily change it into a more empowering belief.

Application with Examples

a) You can convert your limiting beliefs into empowering beliefs and attain that long pending success

Example 1

Limiting belief	Empowering beliefs
I can't drive a car	• If I really want it, I can learn to do anything • Driving is easy if I put my full attention and focus on it

Example 2

Limiting belief	Empowering beliefs
I can't do anything if I don't have money	• Money is a bi-product, if I do the right things with passion, money will flow to me in abundance • I attract success and money • I'm a success magnet • Having more money makes me happy
I can't trust people	• Trust building is a continuous process • I believe every human being has some trustworthy part in them

b) Convert an idea into an empowering belief and make it a big success

Example

IDEA: To sell home-made Jute products online

The Power of Belief

Empowering beliefs

1. I have a natural ability to convince people
2. All that I do with genuine intention result into excellent profits for me
3. I can build a complete empire of my own through my research, action and hard work
4. Right people automatically come to me with right advice at the right time

Think about your goals and write down some empowering beliefs that will help you get energy even when things are not going right.

c) Convert your limiting belief systems about relationships into empowering beliefs

Choose the beliefs that resonate with you the most, and repeat them in your mind, write them down as many times as possible, till the time your brain completely accepts it as a belief.

Limiting beliefs	Empowering beliefs
It is difficult for me to trust people	I trust the larger good in people and universe
	I don't doubt people's intention unless they give me a chance to do that
	I attract like-minded and trustworthy people in my life
	My relationships are blessed with abundance of trust, respect and happiness
I rub people the wrong way most of the times	People love my honesty
	I am always conscious about what is the appetite of the person to listen
	I communicate to be understood
	I have the ability to change my style of communication with different types of people
	For me relationships are important, and I maintain respect and dignity of both me and others in my relationships
People take advantage of me if I get too close to them emotionally	I am smart enough to know when to say NO
	I know when, where and with whom to draw the line
	I trust my intuition/gut to know when to stop
	I am honest in my relationships and communicate openly in case I feel I'm being taken for granted

Limiting beliefs	Empowering beliefs
If I'm honest, my close ones will get hurt and might leave me	All my relationships are mature enough to understand my honest nature
	I like honesty in relationships both ways
	There are times when I choose to stay quite than be honest – and I'm ok with that till it doesn't hurt me or the other person
	If they leave me for my honesty, I'm sure one day they will get matured, understand and come back, I'll choose to wait, rather than dealing with a dishonest relationship
	I know how to communicate my point of view with honesty alongwith taking care of other person's emotions
If I give feedback to my boss/management, they will get back at me	I know when, where and how to give feedback
	The intent of my feedback to boss/management is to serve the best interest of the organization
	I have the ability to provide feedback in a way that it is taken positively and in spirit
	Sometimes when things are ambiguous, it is ok to be quite, and trust the management/boss
	People at work love my fearless, yet respectful attitude

Summary | Chapter 5

Belief system play a major role in how we behave and react to different situations. Our relationships also get impacted owing to our belief systems.

Belief systems largely create the culture and societies.

Limiting beliefs can always be re-programmed. Some of the most common examples in personal and work life are provided in the chapter.

Reader Reflections

1. What are certain limiting beliefs that you have regarding relationships at work or life?

   Here are some most common that I encountered during coaching sessions –

   a. Bosses/clients are there to make life hell for the team

   b. People usually misunderstand me

   c. I need to work extra hours, so people know about my hard work

   d. I can't network with people at work, I have way too much work

   e. I just can't get along with these kind of people

2. List down these limiting beliefs, and question the sanctity, origin and commonality of these beliefs with successful people, your idols etc. Do they share the same belief?

3. Now write down at-least 10 empowering beliefs that will help you build great relationships at work and life.

4. Now give power to these new empowering beliefs by reading, writing these every day, till your brain completely accept them.

06

Dealing with Difficult Relationships

Winning mindset that helps deal with relationships that you can't avoid

Aren't there times when there are people who are close to us, we like them, we love them, but still don't get along with them.

Example me and my best friend, we have known each other from 20 years now, shared our darkest deepest truths, but still ended up into a bad spat after every few years. I felt she was wrong, and she felt I was wrong always!

I noticed a similar thing going in my dad and brother's relationship. Both thought they were right! Oh! And don't start about bosses:)… I always knew bosses were wrong and I was always right.

With subordinates – aaah… I know they don't know as much as me, I have experience, so they better respect that.

And last but not the least, in-laws! How can they ever be right?

Can you connect with anything written above? Do you have a person in your life with whom you share a connection, but you can't just stand him/her?

You put all your efforts to get back in the right spirit of relationship, but just then, again you realize that you don't agree and feel bad when you are around him/her.

Sometimes, the relationship goes well with distance and occasional "hellos," but when you get in touch again, you end up in a fight and emotional outburst, or heaviness in the heart.

You feel that the relationship is either – indispensable- or incredibly close - or at the soul level, but you feel burdened and unhappy with his/her behavior. He/She could be your spouse, boss, subordinate, parents, in-laws, childhood friend anyone!

Brain Codes

In the last few years, I practiced consciously and figured out some incredible brain codes. These brain codes not only helped me mend my relationships with the close ones, but also gave me a new emotional freedom. A freedom where I feel empowered and close to everyone I meet. I'm at a place in life, where I can confidently say that I'm incredibly in love with everyone I meet!

These brain codes are applicable anywhere – at work, home, institutions etc. The more you use them, the more you will feel the freedom and love it.

Brain Codes for Relationships

To start with, here are some *simple empowering beliefs that can change the meaning and essence of your relationships:*

Brain Code 1: People CAN have different definitions of "Right" or "Wrong"

A big reason why we get into an argument is, when we feel we are right and the other person is wrong.

Now, to take it further, there are 3 big reasons why people view the same thing differently –

1. *Different societal rules and cultures*: A westerner might feel public hugging and kissing is right between a man and a woman, while our rural India believe it's a sin
2. *Different circumstances*: A person under huge debt might feel that asking for money and favors is his last resort and is ok, while the others who are well nourished might feel that it is below dignity

3. *Different personality types*: A person might have an extrovert personality and feel that sharing personal information openly is absolutely ok, while the introvert one might feel its too personal and one shouldn't share with everyone

In case, there's someone with a different thought process, here are the possible reactions.

NO. 1: We get in a passionate mode to make the person believe in our thought process, to prove our point, to ensure that the person moves according to us. The intention could be anything – "To make them realize that we are right," or "To make their lives better," or "To make them realize their mistakes and make them better.". etc.

NO. 2: We choose to ignore and sulk, vent it out else where, talk about how wrong the person is doing, but don't tell him/her directly because he/she doesn't listen and won't understand.

> "Most of the times, it's not only the content (*What* you are saying) bothers the other person in a conversation that turns into an argument, it is largely about the process (*How* are you saying) that matters."

Dealing with Disagreements

In times of disagreements, or arguments, there are three key basic constructs that needs to be set right. Let's discuss these below:

1. **Respect**

We don't know where the other person is coming from. What is the experience deep within them, which is making them talk something that we don't agree with. We don't even have time, need and patience to dig deeper.

So, the best thing we can do in this case is, to take a "Short cut." Just trust the fact that the person has the right intentions for himself at-least. And respect the fact that he/she is sharing some opinion. Remember respect here doesn't mean you agree to his/her point of view.

Brain Code 2: Disagreement doesn't mean Disrespect

If we say NO or disagree, the other person will feel that we are disrespecting them. This fear is very prevalent specially in Indian Culture, where most of the kids weren't allowed to speak their minds.

Dealing with Difficult Relationships

I'm blessed to have a dad, who always encouraged a straight talk. Irrespective of any age I go back to – 6yrs till date.

This discussion included how at different point in times, I felt he was wrong and he felt I wasn't doing the right thing.

He always listened to my point of view very patiently, respected it, stated his reasons and closed the conversation amicably.

But I'm well aware of our cultural nuance – where children dare to say NO to their parents. Disagreements meant being disrespectful.

One of the reasons, children lack self-esteem is because their point of views are not respected or even considered.

> "You can respect the other person's point of view, state your own point of view, and can still agree to disagree."

Language like below can help you use the above formula:

- *I respect your point of view, what I understand you said is ...., here's where I'm coming from ...., you don't necessarily have to agree to my point of view*
- *Let's respect each other's point of view and see where we can find a common ground*
- *Lets' leave it here and agree to disagree*
- *Lets' decide basis what is good for the larger cause*
- *While we have given our point of views, let the decision authority take the decision basis what works best according to them*

Role of Intention

The moment our intention changes in between the argument, i.e.

- to defeat the other person, or
- make ourselves look more intelligent, or
- to ensure that it's my way or highway to show the power,

Intention can be sensed by everyone else other than us through our tone and revengeful feelings.

In that case even if the decision goes our way and others agree, we lose some amount of respect.

I'm sure you can recall some news journalists facilitating debates as an example in this case. Recently few of them just lost their respect due to this reason.

2. Judgment

A yet deeper reason why we find it difficult to respect someone is our "Judgment" about the person.

Given below are few scenarios, notice what comes to your mind after reading each of them –

- We look at some old parents living alone, while the children have all the amenities to get them to stay with them, but that doesn't happen
- We look at a person who is in a lot of debt, but is smiling, jumping around with new clothes and phone
- We read flaming e-mails from a person for small little things that can be usually ignored
- A person is shouting at a lady for overtaking him
- A child is crying blatantly in the arms of maid, and the mother rushes to office for an urgent meeting
- A person is non-stop just talking in the meeting, without giving a chance to anyone to speak

Our brain finds all the above situations very stimulating/challenging and starts to process this information to pass on a judgment.

Some common examples of the judgments we make are:

- What an irresponsible and selfish person
- This person is so irresponsible and spendthrift
- She is a big drama queen
- Oh! What a male chauvinist pig
- What an irresponsible mother
- This person is so irritating and full of himself
- He is the most careless person I've seen in life

I remember this one day, I went to my friend's house, she just delivered a baby, her mother was also there sitting with us and chatting. In between, my friend commented about my daughter – "Touch Wood! She seems to have gained weight"

Listening to this, immediately, her mom pitched in with her divine judgmental statement. Ouch! It hurt bad, but what to do…

She said "Whatever you say, you all go to your jobs, and the kid is left behind, how will she get fed the right way?"

It did burn me inside out, and all my guards were up to pick up this battle, well, I have my kid's grandparents staying with us who take care of her, possibly better than I do, she has the best of food habits without any junk intake, we earn so that she gets the best of education and development, we give her more than enough dedicated time and attention every day! Blah blah blah…

Because I was being judged as a bad mother, it was very easy for me to judge this aunty as "Another old fashioned taunting aunty," or "Sadist woman who don't empathize with other women" or "Heartless and insensitive woman who doesn't care about how other person will feel."

I managed to control and just passed on a smile. Forcibly pushed these judgments back, and told myself – "it's just another opinion and point of view… I don't have to let it seep inside me"

But I know, many working women go through this feeling of guilt, defense, helplessness, selfishness and what not, almost every day. If not, some people make them go through this.

Key to managing your reaction is, next time whenever these judgements come to your mind, while talking to someone or through observations, here's a counter empowerment belief that will come to your rescue:

Brain Code 3: We are no-one to judge other person's life or mental state. Let's discount their intention.

When our brain successfully makes a judgment (specially a negative one), it becomes very difficult to "RESPECT" others.

Example: If I've already made a judgment that a person is a male chauvinist pig, I will not be able to "respect" him in any situation for anything.

So the best way to come out of this situation and experience the freedom of love is to "*Replace these judgments with Code 3.*"

This specific dialogue with self, really helps:

> "They have their own point of view, their own personality, their own way of living. We can reflect only on *our* own behavior and reactions"

A famous story explains this beautifully. The scorpion and the frog.

A scorpion asks a frog to carry it across a river. The frog hesitates, afraid of being stung, but the scorpion argues that if it did so, they would both drown. Considering this, the frog agrees, but midway across the river the scorpion does indeed **sting** *the frog, dooming them both. It is in the nature of Scorpion to sting!*

If I were the frog in the story, I would have weighed the facts and would have decided accordingly. Frog is the only one responsible for its outcome and let us refrain from making judgments for both scorpion and frog.

By continuously repeating code 3, not only will you feel less burdened, but also, you will feel the freedom and happiness within you for being a good human being. Try it out!

3. Detachment from "the other person's outcome"

I personally experienced and practiced this formula, and it is just amazing how things in life become simpler.

There was a time when I had become very possessive about my parents. They were in a different city, but in my mind I had taken their complete responsibility. For their health, for their living, for everything they did, I felt responsible and took charge. Even if they told me about a little fever that they had, I use to start feeling helpless and scold them for not taking care of themselves. Would arrange for all kinds of medical tests, and make them eat all that was diet and different than what they were used to. It came to a point that they stopped telling me anything. I came to know later that my mom had an accident, but no one told me because I would have felt stressed.

Next time when we met, in one of our open conversations, when I was yelling at my dad for not telling me anything they went through, he told me how miserable he felt when I reacted to small little things earlier. I was taken aback. My intentions were good. everyone knew, but still they felt choked!

It was a warning call, I thought about it a lot and that's when I realized that "I am not responsible for what happens to them." All I can do is to provide them with the best amenities and resources. They are two individuals leading a life on their own terms with their own style. They take care of each other in the way they like.

Brain Code 4 : At the most, we can suggest, or help or provide resources, but after that what the other person do, is their life and decision and their consequences and we need to RESPECT that.

Yes, my being possessive for them and my behavior to control them, was very disrespectful. I apologized and got back to normal life. I still love them, provide them with all my support and be there with them when they need, but now – I don't control their lives!

> **"Following your desire to "CONTROL" others and make them Think, Believe and Do according to what you think is "RIGHT"… is one of the biggest mistake we do in a relationship."**

In order to break-free from the burden of relationships, and move towards a freedom of love where every person you meet, you fall in love with, one needs to change some core *limiting beliefs to empowering beliefs*.

Also, one needs to really understand the concept of *"Respect," "Impact of Judgment," "Dissociation with outcome"*. That's the only way to love others by taking and giving freedom.

Summary | Chapter 6

Core elements to build WINNING relationships and love everyone you meet -

- Respect
- Refrain from Judgments
- Detachment from "the other person's outcome"

Empowering beliefs

1. People CAN have different definitions of "Right" or "Wrong"
2. Disagreement doesn't mean Disrespect
3. We are no-one to judge other person's life or mental state. Let's discount their intention
4. They have their own point of view, their own personality, their own way of living. We can reflect and make judgments on and for only ourselves
5. At the most, we can suggest, or help or provide resources, but after that what the other person do, is their life and decision and their consequences and we need to RESPECT that

Readers Reflections

1. List down some difficult yet close relationships that you have
2. With every person's name, write down any judgments you have about him/her
3. Are there any limiting beliefs that you have about this relationship?
4. Do you currently feel responsible or owner of their lives? Or outputs?
5. What additional insights do you have now, to make things better?

07

Happiness Redefined

Before searching for it, define what it is to be happy for you?

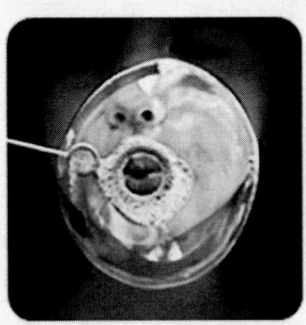

I was profusely in tears, had shut myself in the bathroom. Though I was just 6–7 years old, I still remember this incident so vividly. My dad was knocking the door and requesting me to come out. After a couple of minutes, I opened the door and hugged him tight.

A few minutes ago, I was fighting with mom to get me a new doll, and with all her honesty, she explained why we couldn't buy it. Dad's business was in pits, we barely had food to eat, there were so many people we had borrowed money from, buying a doll was a distant dream. I was shocked to hear this brutal truth and went running to the bathroom to cry it out.

Sobbing and feeling terrible within, I said sorry that I had troubled him so much for buying me things. I told him that I didn't know that we were going through so much otherwise I would have never asked.

He smiled and asked me to look into his eyes, I tried hard to do that and when I did, he said *"Have you ever seen me crying or breaking down? Have you ever seen me sad? Yes, we are going through a tough phase, but that doesn't mean we don't enjoy or be happy! God is with us and this phase will pass by"*

I recollected, how he was always cheerful and greeted guests with all his energy and enthusiasm, how he played with us for hours after coming back from work, how he heard out my school stories giving all the reactions I needed. Our little games on the bed, stories, singing bhajans, eating together, reciting poems and mantras just before going to sleep!

How on the earth I would ever know our situation? How would anyone know? I never saw him hopeless till date, he is always filled with gratitude and an endless zest to live life!

Now when I look back, I feel blessed to get those attributes through genes, perhaps. And while growing up I learnt some more powerful concepts and facts about "Happiness" that further changed my whole life and perspectives.

In this chapter, I will attempt to give some relevant examples and techniques to internalize these concepts.

Remember, even the awareness about these concepts bring a lot of internal transformations in people, so read it with an open mind.

3 Most Important Facts about "Happiness"

1. Happiness Is a State of Mind, It Is Not Correlated with Circumstances

This was my first lesson of life. No matter what we are going through, happiness is a choice.

Even when we weren't doing well, we barely had food to eat, or money for our school fee, but still, we enjoyed and made some amazing childhood memories.

> "When you are going through a tough time, the most natural reaction of the brain is to make you feel negative. The intention of your brain is to push you to take action. Brain will process the threat information and show you all the things that can go wrong."

With that, starts the chain reaction. When you think about what can go wrong, you will feel negative emotions like fear, sadness, embarrassment etc. This gets into a spiral which eventually might lead to depression or feeling low.

Happiness Redefined

So what do we do when we know we are getting into the spiral?

When you start feeling bad or negative, here are some quick tricks you can use, to change the way you are feeling about your circumstance.

1. Learn and repeat these empowering beliefs by heart -
   - ✓ For me, whatever happens, happens for good and happens for a reason that we don't know and might never know
   - ✓ There's always an alternate way to turn around the situation
   - ✓ It's only during the difficult circumstances, we show our true character & personality to ourselves and others who look up-to us
   - ✓ Confusion is good. It means we are moving towards making a substantial change in life
   - ✓ Circumstances are just a phase that passes by. Just ask yourself if you can do something about it. If yes, then do it and don't worry, if no, then anyway don't waste your time worrying! It's as simple as that
   - ✓ My guiding angels are always there to protect me
   - ✓ My intuition in tough times, give me right signals to take best decisions
2. It's "OK" to be sad at times or feel disappointed with the circumstances, the trick is how soon we get out of that sadness and bounce back with double power and energy.
3. Affirmations about "What we really want in a situation?" helps me stay positive and hopeful, instead of cribbing about why it's not there, or not happening.

2. Everyone's Definition of "Happiness" Can Be Different, What's Yours?

My whole life till few years ago, was about fighting it out, get to the top in career, compete and prove myself to others.

I thought I'll be happy after that. I thought, my "happiness" will be when I'll be able to show off to the world that "I've done it"... I did that!... I have that dream house, dream car, more money than them, better lifestyle than them!

Now, that I really did it, got a dream job, dream salary, I felt very shallow. Throughout life I've been chasing these dreams by working really hard, I remember all the stress, conflicts, learnings, reflections, feedback, hurt and pain... but now when I reached life's key milestone – I felt shallow. I realized that it was NOT my true happiness. I've been living in this stress for almost entire life.

With a little more reflection, I realized, my real happiness was in making a difference in other people's lives. Whenever someone came back to me saying that they felt good and their lives changed after talking to me – that's when I felt "Happy" in the real sense. Be it my parents, my friends, my family, relatives or neighbors.

While it is important to have my career for my own self-esteem, credibility and material dreams, I can still choose to be happy throughout the journey, if I clearly know "What makes me happy?." Not for anything else, but only for making a difference and be really happy!

What is it for you? What's your passion that makes you happy?... I realized mid-life crisis for most, is nothing but this!

A redefining phase, a phase when one is confused and figuring out "What real happiness means to him/her?" – And, you bet! It's not an easy task for everyone to identify passion. Blessed are those who are able to identify "What makes them happy," and super blessed are those who are able to change course of life and align more to their happiness.

Here's an attempt you can make to identify your passion. Get a paper pen and answer the following questions –

1. If time and money was not a constraint, what would you have "done?"
2. To the answer of point 1:: What is important about doing that?
3. How much and what does "doing that" mean to you?
4. What will happen if you do that?
5. How will you feel when you do that?
6. Who do you want to see with you, when you are doing that?
7. What are the steps that you can take today, to do that?

I hope you get to find your passion through these questions!

NOTE: What is important to understand here is that, in your ecosystem, every person (your wife, husband, daughter, friends, parents etc.) might have different answers to Question no. 1. above. You need to understand, respect and support them for their passion, if they don't know, help them identify their passion. It might not be same as

Happiness Redefined

yours, but the feeling of happiness attached to it, is the same. This will enable others to support you for your passion as well.

3. We Create Our Own "Happiness" Variables – It's the Game of Our Own Mind!

This last fact, is perhaps the final and the most important key to happiness.

Sometimes, consciously or unconsciously we tag our happiness state with external situations or people or even passion.

The fact is: The more we tag our happiness to the outside world, the more dependent we become, the more susceptible to hurt we are.

When we are in a blame frame, we make ourselves feel pity on us. It's all a game that our mind plays,to make us feel like a victim, because in a victim zone we are safe from the outside world blaming us for things.

Few examples to understand this better -

   a) *Often when I meet Indian newly married couples, specially the wives have this issue. My husband cares more for his parents, or goes out with his friends and forgets me, or doesn't change his lifestyle etc. etc.,*

   b) *He/She didn't call me,*

   c) *They should have respected us,*

   d) *They didn't show any courtesy like we did,*

   e) *The temperature here is so bad,*

   f) *I can't stand their lifestyle etc. etc.*

The question is – Can we re-program our mind to choose different variables for our happiness?

Tried and Tested Recipes for More Happiness

1. Figuring out your passion and spending more time on it will make you forget half of your life's issues. You will find them very petty once you get busy doing what you love!

2. A psychological verbal contract in relationships really helped set expectations.

3. Dissociate with the emotions attached to a situation that couldn't be changed. Concentrate more on the 90% of situations that you can influence or change.

4. Limit the no. of people who impact your happiness quotient (Inner circle). Concentrating on very few close relationships and giving more time and energy to those few relationships will help get more meaning and support.

5. Last but not the least – "A Gratitude list" will keep you happy, enjoy small pleasures and grounded always!

Summary | Chapter 7

Facts about happiness

1. Happiness is a state of mind, it is not correlated with one's circumstances
2. Everyone's definition of "Happiness" can be different
3. We create our own "Happiness" variables – It's the game of our own mind

Readers Reflections

Few questions to identify your passion

1. What is it that you do, gives you real happiness?
2. When was the last time you did it?
3. What can you do today, to do that stuff more and more?
4. What subject could you read 500 books about without getting bored?
5. What could I do for five years straight without getting paid?
6. What would I spend my time doing if I had complete financial abundance to do anything?

If still there is nothing that comes to your mind, remember there's always a right time for things.

Having no passion is also OK, going with the flow, one day at a time, is an art that very few people have. Enjoy the journey as it comes, till you find your purpose.

08

Managing Our Reactions

What would your life look like if you were able to manage your reactions? How free would you feel if you lived your life by choice? If these questions energize you, then you will love this chapter.

Sometimes it becomes just impossible to manage our emotions and we react instantly to most likely regret later. What are those triggers that just take over the whole grip on your emotions and behaviors? How can we re-program those triggers and change our reactions?

Let's look into it in more details in this chapter.

What Are Triggers?

Triggers are those moments/events/topics, that touch some part of your emotional brain. You immediately start feeling emotions in your body and mind. These can be positive or negative.

For example: Key in the car is used as a trigger to switch it on or off. We know that there is a lot of hardware and complete process installed inside the car which gets initiated by just putting in the key in to start the car.

Similarly, an external trigger is enough to start a huge internal process that is pre-programmed in our brain, and we feel that we have no control on what happens next. It's automatic!

In my umpteen number of programs in and outside India, wherever I went I asked this question –

"A" for? *and 99.9% of the times the answer that came out was APPLE.*

Here, A for? Is a trigger to a rehearsed response – APPLE

Examples of positive triggers: Someone who brought a gift for you, a surprise, an unexpected call from a close one, a gratitude from someone, appreciation, rewards, recognition and many more.

Examples of negative triggers:

- Someone leaving you (or the threat that they will).
- Someone rejecting you.
- Helplessness over painful situations.
- Someone discounting or ignoring you.
- Someone being unavailable to you.
- Someone giving you a disapproving look.
- Someone blaming or shaming you.
- Someone being judgmental or critical of you.
- Someone being too busy to make time for you.
- Someone not appearing to be happy to see you.
- Someone coming on to you sexually in a needy way.
- Someone trying to control you.
- Someone being needy, or trying to smother you.

The fact is that positive and negative triggers can be different for different people, basis their experiences, meanings and translations they assigned to certain things/events etc.

For example, I was watching a tv reality show and this particular contestant who was otherwise quite patient, active and mature, got extremely agitated with a single sentence: "You are a Smart player" – later she regretted her behavior, but the word "Smart" just touched some chord and she got into a reactive mode. No one could understand what was so rude about this word, whether it was worth making such a big ruckus, but the fact is that – it was her "trigger."

Yes – words are also triggers.

Identifying the Source of Our Triggers

There are several reasons behind our triggers, sometimes only understanding the origin of the trigger can resolve the whole reaction issue.

1. A simple unconscious generalization (unexplained belief without facts) in our mind, which was created years ago (maybe in childhood) by mere listening or reading about something, can evoke a trigger.

Example: **Women are bad drivers on the road** – immediately if you see a woman driving a car ahead of you and she suddenly applies a break, your reaction will be much different than how it will be, if that was a normal male driver.

2. When we were growing up, we inevitably experienced pain or suffering that we could not acknowledge and/or deal with sufficiently at the time. So as adults, we typically become triggered by experiences that are reminiscent of these old painful feelings. As a result, we typically turn to a habitual or addictive way of trying to manage the painful feelings.

Example case 1: Julie (name changed) was raised by absent parents. Her father traveled frequently, and her mother was emotionally unavailable. She was left alone a lot even as a toddler, and when her sister was born two years later, Maddie was put in charge of her. By age five, Maddie was not only in charge of making meals for herself, but also her sister and their younger brother. She essentially raised herself.

Today, Julie is a very competent physician, but she gets painfully triggered when someone she cares about isn't available. When she calls her daughter at college and her daughter doesn't return the call, Julie gets upset and sometimes even begins to blame her husband for her pain (even though it has nothing to do with him).

Until Julie began her work with me, she didn't realize that "unavailability" is her trigger, and that she most often tries to avoid her old pain by blaming her husband. But now that she is aware of the trauma from her childhood neglect, Julie is learning to compassionately attend to her inner child in order to heal.

Example case 2: I was the youngest of my 4 siblings. Out of 4 of us, 2 of my sisters were adopted by my 2 paternal uncle/aunts. While I was growing up, I always saw my mom closer to my sisters who were far away from her, she evidently gave more attention, care, gifts and showered all her attention to them when they visited us, so much so, that she'd almost forget my existence. I use to feel very neglected, jealous and would do all kind of stuff to gain her attention. This went on for years.

I grew up to be very possessive about the people I loved. The issue came after marriage when I made my husband's life hell even if he passed a smile or message to any other girl, he was completely banned to talk unnecessarily to any girl except me, even in office! I always thought it is a natural jealousy

Managing Our Reactions

and I'm jealous because I loved him, until it started choking him and I spoke about this problem with my coach.

I realized, my trigger was "sharing my loved one with someone else" in any way. The unconscious hurt in the childhood owing to my mom ignoring me in the presence of my sisters, had made me very insecure and possessive about my loved ones.

The moment I realized, I consciously worked on it, reframed the incidents, and reprogrammed my mind to be ok and secured.

My husband is surely very happy now 😊

3. Sometimes, you react when you feel as though you aren't getting or will not get one of these needs met -

- ✓ acceptance
- ✓ respect
- ✓ be liked
- ✓ be understood
- ✓ be needed
- ✓ be valued
- ✓ be in control
- ✓ be right
- ✓ be treated fairly
- ✓ attention
- ✓ comfort
- ✓ freedom
- ✓ peacefulness
- ✓ balance
- ✓ consistency
- ✓ order
- ✓ predictability
- ✓ love
- ✓ safety

- ✓ feel included
- ✓ autonomy
- ✓ fun
- ✓ new challenges
- ✓ independence

Choose three items from the list that most often set off your emotions when you don't get these needs met. Be honest with yourself. Which three needs, when not met, will likely trigger a reaction in you? Identify the needs that you hold most dear.

So, two things we need to understand about triggers are –

1. Everyone has a trigger that evokes series of emotions and reactions in them. It's like our brain has programmed – when this happens – I will feel like this – I will react like this

2. Triggers can be different for different people, based on their experiences, cultures etc.

Typical Reactions to Common Triggers

In a natural unconscious setting, given below are the typical reactions that we resort to –

- Get angry
- Get needy
- Comply. Become a people-pleaser
- Shutdown and withdraw from the other person
- Blame someone else for my pain
- Turn to an addiction – food, drugs, alcohol, sex, porn, shopping, work gambling and so on

Dealing with Triggers

Tools to re-program our reactions to positive responses

Unless you re-program your response to that trigger, the brain will always flawlessly work on the pre-programmed reactions. To begin with lets' understand the difference between a reaction and a response -

Managing Our Reactions

Reaction: Instant & unfiltered natural feelings and behavior which is not thought through

Response: A thought through action for a trigger, which eventually elicits constructive feelings

There was a time when I just could never deal with someone being rude to me. I inadvertently would cry and feel very angry, later would regret and hate myself for that reaction! This had become a phenomena, until one of my managers coached me and made me think about "How would I react next time if it happens"

> *"I rehearsed that new reaction in my mind so many times, that when the situation came next time, automatically my reaction had changed to a thought through response."*

I was elated and very proud of myself.

However, remember that this change from reaction to response is gradual.

There might be times you might slip into the old pattern, but be "OK" with it. Give your brain some time to completely re-program. What is more important is to check whether the frequency of your responses is increasing than the frequency of your reaction.

Earlier, out of 10 times if you'd react 9 times, now has it reduced to 6 or 7 times? That's how it works and you need to be ok with the speed your brain is accepting your new programming. You will eventually get to a total 10 out of 10 response time instead of reaction! Just keep at it and be ok even if you slipped couple of times.

Tool 1: Activity | Self-Reflection

1. While everyone has number of triggers, think about that one trigger which brings the worst in you.
2. What do you think is the origin of that trigger?
3. What do you do when you encounter that trigger? How do you feel?
4. What would you want to do next time if the same trigger happens? How do you want to feel?

    (Preferably write these answers, and replay the answer of 3rd point at-least 2–3 times a day in your mind to re-program)

Notice the magic of this exercise, once you experience the trigger next time 😊

Tool 2: Given below Are 5 Steps to Manage the Emotional Triggers

Remember to follow these steps, when you are in a neutral productive mood, this is not to be followed when you are in midst of your emotional reaction.

1. **Accept that you are responsible for your reaction**

   If you have a trigger that makes you angry or brings out an unwanted reaction, the primary task is to accept it. Shielding it with reasons, rationalizing behavior will only make you feel victim inside. Remember it's a sign of the brave one, to accept the issue and get ready to deal with it, especially if it is deep and personal.

2. **Recognize the emotional reaction**

   Now that you know a little more about your trigger, reflect on how you feel in your body when the trigger is evoked. Recognize the process that's happening within your body, think about the **physiological signals**. For example, the moment I realize someone is talking to me rudely, my throat starts choking and I immediately recognize the pattern. What is yours, when you encounter your trigger?

3. **Determine the source of the trigger**

   While it might be time taking or little intense, start reflecting through your life and identify what could be the possible trigger? Refer to earlier section about identifying the source of the trigger.

   One of my coachee was very upset owing to his aggressive reactions to slip-ups from any of his team members. After reflections, he realized that unconsciously he was following his mom's pattern for perfection and would get upset if his perfection criteria wasn't met. A mere realization of the source of his trigger, immediately changed his reaction and aggression to a positive response for life.

4. **Choose a new response and feeling for that trigger**

   With practice, the reaction to your emotional triggers could subside, but they may never go away. The best you can do is to quickly identify when an emotion is triggered and then choose what to say or do next. Mentally play the whole scenario with the new reaction. Describe vividly the whole scenario as many times as it takes to internalize it.

Ask yourself: Are you really losing this need or not? Is the person actively denying your need or are you taking the situation too personally? If it's true that someone is ignoring your need or blocking you from achieving it, can you either ask for what you need or, if it doesn't really matter, can you let the need go for now?

Choose to ask for what you need, or let it go if you honestly feel that asking for what you need will have no value, or do something else to get your need met.

5. **Consciously shift your emotional state**

   When you determine your response to a trigger, shift into the emotion that will help you get the best results.

   ✓ Relax – breathe and release the tension in your body.

   ✓ Detach – clear your mind of all thoughts, and imagine you are looking at the situation from the ceiling that is 30ft high.

   ✓ Center – drop your awareness to the center of your body just below your navel.

   ✓ Focus – choose one keyword that represents how you want to feel in this moment. Breathe in the word and allow yourself to feel the difference.

Tool 3: Re-Program Your Brain for Reactions

Identify your triggers for "reactions" or bad feelings

Our "reactions" to a particular stimulus are pre-programmed, examples –

1. I feel vulnerable, when my daughter falls ill
2. I feel very angry and can't control my tears, when someone shouts at me
3. I feel sad and depressed every-time I see or hear an ambulance

Now, if only you take your 5 minutes right now and jot down at-least 5 most common identifiable triggers, you will be able to drastically get down the no. of times you feel bad –

1. I feel _____, when _____
2. I feel _____, when _____
3. I feel _____, when _____
4. I feel _____, when _____
5. I feel _____, when _____

Now, you need to change the above statements into commands to your brain.

For better understanding, given below are few examples -

> **Trigger 1: I feel vulnerable, when my daughter falls ill**
>
> *Command 1:* Next time when my daughter falls ill, I will feel the strength in me to take care of her, she needs a stronger mother, and I'm the one for her.

> **Trigger 2: I feel very angry and can't control my tears, when someone shouts at me**
>
> *Command 2:* Next time when someone is shouting at me, I will remind myself that the saner one is that, who doesn't react immediately out of emotions. I will take my time and behave like a matured adult

> **Trigger 3: I feel sad and depressed every-time I see or hear an ambulance**
>
> *Command 3:* Next time when I see or hear an ambulance, I will pray for the person in it, and feel gratitude for all that I have today

Tool 4: Identify Your Command Zone

Think about all the issues, challenges and worries that you currently hold in your life. List down all of them without any inhibitions:

Managing Our Reactions

1.
2.
3.
4.
5.
6.
7.
8.
9.
10.

Now in front of each of the above sentence, think carefully and answer this question

1. Is it in your control?(Yes/No)
2. What can you do about it today/tomorrow? (Something/Nothing)

   Write a "Yes" and the action that you should take or Write a "No" against each one of them listed above.

Interpretation

If the number of "No" are more than "Yes"… what does it tell you? You are right now in a situation of life, where most of the challenges/issues are not in your direct control or influence.

Similarly, if the number of "Yes" are more than "No"… what does it tell you? Perhaps you don't know how to or where to start, or when will it end.

In any of the above case, remember one thing – "The only one thought process that brings peace, success and action to our lives is – to focus your 90% of the day on stuff that is in your control or influence."

Here's a quick summary to this –

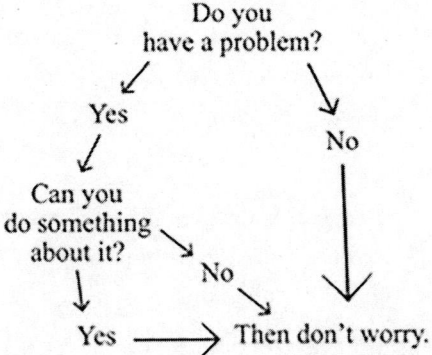

Time is the most precious thing one has. The best way to manage your time, emotions and energy is to – "Spend maximum amount of time on things that are in your command zone." There is no point thinking and brooding over things that you can do nothing about! It's not even worth picking it up over tea/coffee – gossips.

I love what Stephen Covey said in his book – "7 habits of highly effective people." 10% of what happens in our life is destiny (we have no control over it whatsoever) and depending on how we react to that 10%, rest of the 90% of life takes shape.

We can choose to either sit over it, cry and vent out on several people, till we get sympathies and feel content, or we can choose to "make the best out of what is remaining." It's a CHOICE.

Summary | Chapter 8

- **Triggers** are those moments/events/topics, that touch some part of your emotional brain. You immediately start feeling emotions in your body and mind. These can be positive or negative.

- **Facts** about triggers
  - ✓ Everyone has a trigger that evokes series of emotions and reactions in them. It's like our brain has programmed – when this happens – I will feel like this – I will react like this
  - ✓ Triggers can be different for different people, based on their experiences, cultures etc.

- **Sources of negative triggers**
  - ✓ Unconscious generalization
  - ✓ Unresolved childhood experiences
  - ✓ Unmet needs

- **Common reaction to triggers** include depression, anger, avoidance and some other similar unwanted behaviors

- **Dealing with triggers**
  - ✓ Pre-programming our response to specific negative triggers
  - ✓ A 5 – step model to work on our reactions and handle emotions intelligently
  - ✓ Re-program your triggers
  - ✓ Identify your command zone

09

Intentions: Did You Really Mean That?

"**B**ut why the hell did you go out if you weren't well?" - shouted Aliya at her husband!

"Don't you get it, I had to give my phone for repair, else I would have lost a big client deal" - exclaimed Satish who was sneezing and burning with fever. "It wasn't that bad at that time anyway, else I wouldn't have gone!"

Silence for a couple of minutes followed with a huge quarrel. All the last 5 married years details were discussed - how irresponsible Satish was, how work was the only thing on his head all the time, how many times he ignored Aliya because of work! and how accusing and judgmental Aliya was, how nothing was enough for her....!!!

Wait! Can you relate to this scenario above? It might very well happen at work as well. Here's a work example: "Kris, I've been looking at your performance data since last 40 days, and I'm afraid that the results are not as expected. I suggest you start taking your work seriously and spend a little extra time getting trained, so your performance scores are better." - said Rohan with a concerned tone.

"But I thought I was doing ok, if this was the case, why did you not tell me before!" exclaimed Kris.

"I have been in constant touch with the customers, have resolved the most important cases in last 6 months, saved more than $100,000 with my new ideas in the past, and you are telling me to start taking work seriously, just because last 40 days have not been up to the mark? I know my utilization is low, that too because I'm struggling with few things, but that doesn't mean I'm not taking my work seriously or I need some training." – argued Kris with utmost irritation and disappointment on his face

I'm sure all of us have been through this type of conversation before. This chapter talks about a very simple yet powerful conversational technique to make our lives and relationships trustworthy, simpler and peaceful! The catch is to practice it consciously after you know about this technique.

DISCLAIMER: This chapter covers only the simple aspects of conversation to build rapport and relationships at work and home. It doesn't deal with the extremes like - Intention to kill or destroy.

Power of Intention

Most renowned leaders talked about "TRUST" being one of the key factors to build rapport and great relationships. However, TRUST comes with some efforts that we put into a relationship.

Here's my simple technique that works wonders to build trust. I've been practicing it for 85% of the scenarios at home and at work... and it works 100% of the times –

When you have to communicate a difficult message –

1. Shed the Ego - Tell the Truth about Your Intention

Often, we leave the burden of understanding our intention, on the other person. He should understand how much I care for him, or he should know that I'm saying this for his good!

The problem with that approach is, that we assume that we already have the established trust because we are related or know each other for a long time. That's not true! You can be related for years, but "Trust" is never built without talking about our intentions of an action. Why do you think we connect with people on drinks/ informal gatherings much better? It is because, in those gatherings, we shed our ego and talk heart to heart!

Now another problem that I hear from my coachees is, I did tell him about my intention, but next time again he reacted the same way. How many times do I tell? My answer to that is - as many times as he wants to listen. It's always better and emotionally easier to tell the intention rather than reacting and yelling.

> "Why do we feel that ego to NOT tell our intention or how bad we are feeling? What will go wrong if the other person knows that we are feeling hurt, or sad, or disappointed. Confessions like these don't make us vulnerable, they make us stronger, more graceful and authentic!"

Now let's look at the examples quoted above with a different approach to handle -

- Aliya told Satish - "I feel very sad and hurt when you are not well. I can't see you lying sick on the bed, it's very hurtful to see you there." Can you please think about me, before you do this to yourself next time? My intention is to see you healthy and active.

What do you think Satish's reaction will be?

- Kris - I've specially called you for this meeting because I'm concerned about your performance since last 40 days. Intention of this discussion is for us to come up with a plan to ensure that you continue to remain our STAR performer. Let's talk about it and see what both of us can do to enable yours and team's better performance in future.

The more and more we practice this art of telling our intention before the actual content, the more we build trust and rapport with others.

2. Clarify the Intention

If at all you are the recipient in the conversation, it comes very handy to **clarify the intention**. This is a tricky one, especially when you don't have trust or any established relationship.

It is important for you to identify and acknowledge how you are feeling about the first person's comment. Some people lack this ability to put a name to a feeling. *For that I recommend them reading more about emotional intelligence or emotional vocabulary.*

Until a point when you decide to take Sanyas, this emotional vocabulary will help you deal with reactions to most common issues in life.

Here are some examples/statements to clarify the other person's intention.

Example

- Rohan, when you asked me to start taking my work seriously, I felt very disappointed. What exactly did you mean?
- Rohan, when you said that I should spend extra time on training, I felt very uncomfortable. How do you think extra training will help me?

After this, let the other person explain his/her intention. It is important to ask difficult/right questions to help the other person to clarify intentions.

An attempt to understand the other person's underlying intention makes things and consequences much easier to deal with.

Remember Always

- Sometimes, these questions to clarify intentions, can make the other person react further. It's a good sign. Give time for him/her to react or come back. At-least you have made that first attempt to clarify instead of reacting.

- Sometimes, we make a strong presumption that the person's intention is NOT right. In that case, we will never be able to establish trust and rapport, so any attempt to clarify intent or telling the truth will not help! - This is a deeper issue.

- It is advisable to give a benefit of doubt and trust the person's intention when he/she's stating it explicitly and question your own presumptions. Having a heart to heart about how you feel can also help in this case.

Summary | Chapter 9

"Stating your intent" and "Clarifying other person's intent:" these two skills will make you a great conversationalist over a very short span of time.

> **"Please watch out your own intention before getting into this conversation - "It should be to build trust and rapport with the other person and not to prove him/her wrong!"**

Reader Reflections

- It is important to realize that end of the day it is your action/reaction/response that matters
- Meaning of the communication is it's effect, which essentially means, no matter how great your intentions are, if the other person is unable to understand, then your communication has a flaw. You need a smarter way to put across your stuff
- Unless a person explicitly tells you that he/she has bad intentions for you (which happens rarely), trusting other person's intention always gives peace, irrespective of the fact that the person has hurt us

10

Managing Expectations

> *"Expectation is the root of all heartache."*
>
> **– William Shakespeare**

Expectations are a natural process for any human being. We not only expect from others, we expect from our own selves as well.

Expectations range from a meagre – "Thank you" to a superior performance, more salary, respect and so on.

The problem is not the expectations, the real problem starts when these expectations are not met! I've seen people getting worked up, stressed out, cribbing, gossiping and even committing suicide as they couldn't meet expectations – of either self or others, or their own expectations from others weren't met.

In this chapter, we will learn about *4 aspects of expectations* and how we can better manage those.

1. Our expectations from self
2. Our expectations from others
3. Other people's expectations from us
4. Our expectations from life and destiny!

1. Our Expectations from Self

I saw this happening and was totally bewildered. A class topper, scored 97% this time. His friends were as usual elated and were congratulating him, asking him for a treat, but this guy was utterly disappointed and made faces.

He was constantly murmuring something and not looking happy about the scores. When asked about it – he said, "I expected 99%," will need to check what happened."

At work, I saw this happening quite a few times, when despite the fact that the teams attained 99% of the goals, which was unprecedented growth in the history, their manager wasn't happy about the 1% and didn't appreciate the team.

And the best one which is universally accepted truth. I am a reasonably healthy person ☺ delightfully plump as I call myself. However, I've seen perfect shaped girls cribbing about their weight and how they are not happy with some extra pounds or aren't still happy with how they look.

This kind of unhappiness & dissatisfaction with self, further leads to issues not only with self-esteem, but also impacts other people working or living with us. This is quite draining emotionally.

Why Do We Expect from Ourselves so Much?

Before we learn the tools to manage our expectations from self, let's deep dive into how these expectations are built. Root cause of these expectations are deeper and needs to be understood first.

- **Roots in childhood/parenting**

If your parents were too demanding unconsciously* *I'm writing the word unconsciously because I think largely parents don't have a bad intention for their kids and whatever they do is intended for them to be successful.*

They seldom praised you for the achievements small or big and kept asking you to do better and better!

The psychology they possibly had was – if we praise the accomplishment, our child might become complacent or stop putting in more. So, they went overboard, and instead of appreciating they thought it will be better to motivate our child to do more.

However, one thing we as parents need to understand is, that while motivation to do more and get to next level is important for our children, **appreciating** what children have achieved is even MORE important. In addition, appreciating the failures is even more effective to build self-esteem in children.

- **Be Perfect** (Driver)

In a lot of cases, people just don't feel satisfied with their own work till they achieve the highest level of perfection. While in every sense it sounds like a great quality to have, however, in today's word it works as a deterrent to a lot of tasks which really don't need that perfection.

Example: Boss asks you to put together a quick presentation that can be reviewed tomorrow with the larger team, as this is the only chance in next 3 months, that the team will be meeting face to face. While its' your chance to gain boss's trust, you work the entire night to make it perfect, still couldn't share it on time, because as per you, there were some ambiguous points that needed clarification from other teams.

The fact is that your boss just needed one rough draft which had a meaningful outline.

There are times when effectiveness and efficiency is more important than perfection. In today's world, with less time in hand for everything, expecting everything (important as well as not important) you deliver, to be perfect is a recipe for failure.

- **Fear of criticism/feedback/failure**

Deep root for both the reasons mentioned above could be fear of criticism from others.

Because I fear people might criticize, I strive for more and more from myself. I'm running away to save myself from any kind of failure, criticism or feedback.

- **Fear of "Happiness"**

Most commonly I heard from people: "I don't want to be too happy as I heard, the moment one feels happy, or laugh too much, I will get a reason to cry or face difficulties.."

They adopt this belief so close to heart, that they get used to hiding their emotions and not come out openly with appreciation.

Their brain keeps searching the reasons to be unhappy with self and/or others too.

People with high-expectations from themselves may fall into a trap of unhappiness, dissatisfaction and even depression in case they are not able to fulfill those expectations.

Disclaimer: Having high-expectations from self is not bad at all, in fact, it is a potential WINNING attribute in successful people.

Where it gets into a harmful zone is, when they are unable to appreciate their journey, when they fail to balance themselves even when expectations are not met.

> "High expectations from self is great, the difference is whether we respect ourselves and maintain our self-esteem, if the expectation is not met."

Tools to Reduce the Burden of Self-Expectations

Tool 1: Vision and Goals Are Different from Expectations

Can you connect with any of the following thoughts

1. As an entrepreneur, if I spend a lot of time and effort in my business, I should be able to make desired money
2. As a mother, I should be able to take care of my child's health, so he never falls ill
3. My dad has spent so much money for this course, I should get nothing less than 98%
4. I work harder than anyone else in the team, I should get a great hike this year
5. I'm a house wife, I need to ensure that everyone's household needs are met

Now, these are perfect examples of *expectations mixed with goals/vision.*

Having a vision or a goal is great, but we are **setting ourselves up for disappointment** when we couple it with expectations.

To set goals, first step is to write what is in your **direct control** to execute, i.e. **minus the expectations or results**

1. Spend at-least 10 hours a day at work and put in my best abilities to serve my purpose
2. I provide nutritious food and utmost care to my child for a healthy living
3. I aim to study hard and strategize my plan in a way that I score 98% in exams
4. I work hard and compete to produce highest quality and value amongst my team members
5. I set-my schedule and manage household responsibilities to the best of my abilities

While we can have vision that includes outcomes, however, Vision is just an idea about the future. It gives you hope. It tells you what life could be in the future. But vision never gives you a deadline. It can't guarantee it would make you successful. It never even asks you to execute it!

"A vision is meant to give you power to create a desirable future outcome, a *goal is a tangible step within your control* **towards the vision."**

Managing Expectations

Do you think Microsoft CEO – Bill Gates had a guarantee that he will make it THIS big? His vision was to have a computer in every household in the world.

Now, if Mr. Bill Gates had high expectations from himself alongwith the self-critical syndrome mentioned above, he would have been the saddest man on the earth, as despite being a billionaire, one of the richest man on the earth, his vision is still unfulfilled! Not ALL households have a desktop or computer. Think about it, does it really matter so much to him. He did achieve a lot of things while following his vision!

Same case with Amazon (Jeff Bezos) whose vision is "To build a place where people can come to find and discover anything they might want to buy online." – it's a multi-billion dollar company, but can we find everything on Amazon? The answer is no. But does it mean Jeff is not happy! Well, he should be 😊

To sum up, ensure that you are creating a vision that is compelling you to think big and that motivates you to do better, ensure that you follow your goals and keep updating them as you learn on the way to vision, however, the biggest thing you need to ensure is – "detach yourself from the outcome." Like a very famous verse in Geeta says "Karm kar fal ki chinta mat kar" meaning – "Do your duty and don't worry about the outcome"

Tool 2: Acceptance of "Now"

While there is a very enormous benefit of having a vision, this specific step will certainly help you come closer to it.

In my childhood days, we use to live on the top floor of a 2-story building, it had a big balcony where I use to stand, and observe the surroundings, our locality with rich people, cars, dedicated security guards for these huge houses, railway lines at a distance.

We didn't have a car or a colour tv, we had this old-fashioned radio, my dad had a Lamberetta – a very bulky scooter, that made so much noise and embarrassed me so much, that I would never miss my school bus, fearing that I will have to go on that scooter 😊.

I use to see all my friends in that colony with all kinds of amenities, my friends would talk about clubs they went to, and I didn't know what a club was meant for.

One day I was standing in the balcony, observing stuff and thinking about how our life would be, if we had a car, dedicated maids etc. I enjoyed the feeling for some time and started to visualize how I would look driving my own car, how will I feel when have a dedicated room for myself and a house so big that I will feel proud to invite my school friends. It was a great feeling and I was getting goose bumps.

In few minutes, I saw my dad coming from the end of the street in his Lamberetta, heard that loud noise and there you go! Bam! My dream broke, I met the reality, and felt so frustrated that I had tears in my eyes. I could feel the heaviness in my throat and felt miserable and helpless within. My face turned red with blood rush.

My mom noticed and asked the reason. I started yelling – "why are we not so rich, why can't we buy a car, why do we have to struggle so much, while others enjoy!!!"

My dream few minutes ago, became a frustration in no time!

My mom stood by me in the balcony, calmed me down, hugged me and when I felt settled after venting out, she showed me the railway lines and asked me to observe that.

I was surprised I never looked beyond trains. She showed me those small blue hutments where children were playing. There was this huge water tank and it was overflowing, these children barely had clothes on them, didn't have even the slippers, but were dancing under the water fall and enjoying.

She told me that these kids don't even go to school, some help their parents in labor work, some go to houses for cleaning work. They don't have more than 2 pair of clothes, if they fall ill, sometimes they don't have money to go to the doctor.

I knew what mom wanted to tell. She said – ***"Always be thankful for what you have, and then have dreams for what you want"***

That's a lesson that I follow even till date and it gives me happiness to the core.

Today, I live in a different city, posh colony, big car, I have my dream home with all amenities, live-in maid, full time maid, dedicated security guards and systems, and yes, by the way, a great club-house which is a talk of the town!!

I fulfilled my dreams, but look at the co-incidence, we still have those blue hutments right next door, visible from my balcony☺, I am thankful to those, as they keep me grounded and remind me of those magical childhood moments.

I show them to my daughter now.

> **"Having dreams and vision is the first key to success, however, the key to attain that success and true happiness is to be "Grateful" for what you already have in life."**

Managing Expectations

Even if you don't have something that you want badly now, accept the truth gracefully, be "OK" with that, only then you can truly move towards getting it.

Many people say, law of attraction doesn't work for them, and 99% of the times, this is the reason. They don't accept the "NOW" and be truly ok with not having stuff they want.

Tool 3: Play the "Hero," Not the "Victim"

"Wow! What a lovely saree! You look ravishing in it" – said Anita to Sri, and in response Sri cringed and said – "O no, I have gained a lot of inches, so sarees don't suit me anymore, you are being too kind."

"Hey Vinod, your presentation was awesome, you covered all the points so nicely!," said his boss, to which Vinod's response was "No sir, I forgot to mention one in the end, time was too short!."

What do you think is common in the above examples?

The fact is that many of us are not comfortable taking compliments or accepting the goodness in us! Primarily because it contradicts the concept of "humbleness" and humility that we are taught right from our childhood.

This by far is the largest reason, for us to feel victims and depressed, as neither we praise ourselves nor we completely accept positive stroke from others.

The more people praise, the more expectations we raise from ourselves and keep ourselves as VICTIMs, rather than accepting the praises and feel like a HERO.

There is also a scientific reason behind this behavior.

Have you ever thought, despite being much physically weaker than many of the wild animals, how do we survive on the earth longer than most of them?

There are 2 reasons – first – we are social animals and use the power of mass/society, second – our ability to foresee problems and resolve them proactively help us to live more.

> "Our brain, like any other animal, works on the concept of "Survival," hence thinking negative and sensing the danger comes faster and natural to us, instead of thinking about the positives of a situation and accept mental security."

Our brain loves making us a victim, so that we are always on guard. Therefore, if we don't do anything about our thinking process, and let our brain wonder around, it will always bring negative things first and avoid accepting anything positive, it might even show you some danger in the positive coming your way! "Survival" is the core job of the brain- so we can't blame it.

Two nice related quotes that I liked might help you understand and relate to the topic better –

"The truth is, it's more enjoyable to have our negative beliefs reaffirmed than saying something good about ourselves which we don't believe in."

"Negative self-talk offers us some comfort and familiarity because it re-affirms our limiting beliefs about ourselves."

What We Can Do about It?

Reprogram it consciously and explain it to our brain *(remember it takes our commands directly)* that -

1. There is nothing wrong or dangerous about taking "Compliments." Even if you feel the person is not being genuine or have some ulterior motives, still take the compliment gracefully. Give yourself positive strokes and raise your self-esteem to an optimum level.

2. There is an immense power that you will get by accepting the "Qualities and successes" that you've achieved so far. In fact, in today's world, being a "HERO" will save you and help you survive better, then being a "Victim".

Now that you've understood the value and tools to utilize expectations from self in order to win, let's take a closer look at the next part, i.e. how do we manage our expectations from others.

2. Our Expectations from Others

After coaching 1000s of people with varied backgrounds across the world, I realized and learnt one very important lesson.

> "Core to most of our problems today is not the people themselves, it is our own expectations from other people."

Managing Expectations

All of us have our childhood stories, that our parents or close ones love to recite, related to our mischiefs, funny comments, our innocence, our thoughtfulness etc. etc.

This is my favorite memory, my folks laugh at me even today, but it has a big lesson for me, so I love listening to it again and again.

Every-day, the street vendors on cycles or with baskets on their heads, use to come with some exciting stuff for children like sweet potato, star fruits, small play rides etc. They use to have their own unique tone/lines, that they use to call out very loud, so we know they have come.

I loved that stuff and with every shout out, I'd run to my mom and ask for money to buy it. But it was getting difficult for my mom to manage, as I wanted stuff from every vendor.

One day, both my mom dad sat down to explain me why I shouldn't eat stuff from every vendor, but I was very angry and felt helpless, with frustration I told them – *"Tell them not to come to our street from tomorrow, if they come, I will have to eat"* – and I ran away.

While it was simple and amusing answer for my parents, but whenever they talk about this, I keep relating it to 1000's of conversations that I get into with my coachees, who are adults, but come up with a similar issues – "How do I make my wife realize that this thing hurts me!," "How do I tell my husband that he must do this," "Why can't my boss be a little more human to me?"

Their expectation is for others to **not do** or **do** something, not to work other way round.

This is a clear recipe to be unhappy and unsuccessful.

People have expectations like:

My boss will recognize my work performance this month, my wife would appreciate how well I cleaned up the kitchen, my husband will now express his love more etc.

For most of us - Disappointment, irritation, anger, sadness most often arise because others didn't respond in the way we imagined they would.

Rather than looking inward for change, we start expecting from others. And that's what gets us into an emotional trouble. Just like how I use to expect the vendor to not come to our street 😌

Why Do We Expect from Others so Much?

1. **Please others (inner driver)**

    As per the Transactional analysis concept by Eric Berne, one of the drivers that we develop in our childhood is "Please others." People who have this driver as dominant in their personalities, suffer a lot if they don't manage it well.

    In their bid to please others, not only they have high expectations from themselves, but also, because they do so much for others, by going out of their way, that it is natural that they start expecting something in return from others. It could be even a little thank you! If not given back, they feel like a victim.

    My mother-in law(MIL) is extremely giving in nature. She goes out of her way in anything and everything. She cooks for hours in the kitchen instead of going out and enjoying other stuff. Opposite to that is my father-in law(FIL), who loves going out for his walks, spending time with his colony friends, and of course eating great dishes that mom cooks. The catch is, FIL is extremely inexpressive, which leaves my MIL feeling very incomplete. She keeps cribbing all the time for just that one moment of appreciation. While her expectations increased over the years, her frustration and depression also increased, she has already been through couple of heart attacks, has a pacemaker installed.

    Now, even if people appreciate her, go out of the way to let her know that they love her, she doesn't accept it. It is really sad to witness this every day, while no one is at fault.

> "It's these unfulfilled expectations that is killing some people from inside."

2. **Unfulfilled needs and desires**

    There are some basic needs that people are deprived of, the more they realize and miss those things, the more they start expecting from other relationships.

For example, Sammy whose basic need was appreciation at work, had a boss named Veena, who is not expressive at all. The more Sammy saw and heard other bosses appreciate their team members, her expectations started getting exponential from Veena. It became too ugly towards the end, and Sammy left the organization on a very bad and frustrating note.

In another case, John who is known to be a big foody and loves eating all kind of food, got married to Daisy who doesn't know cooking.

Initially things were fine, both were deeply in love with each other. As time passed by, John started noticing his friends, whose spouses were cooking awesome new dishes and posting on Facebook and watsapp groups. He started feeling weird about it and wished his wife did the same.

He started expecting his wife to learn cooking for him and that started a big issue in their otherwise great life.

3. **Insecurities**

   Sometimes we are so insecure about our relationships, that we start expecting others to either prove or show their love to us in different ways and forms.

   This insecurity can stem from any past experience or observation that we might have internalized unconsciously.

   For example, when Sapna realized that the organization she worked for, was looking at cutting down the number of promotions, her insecurities and competitiveness began to increase. She started expecting a lot more from her boss, her team and others at work. Eventually, looking at this immature behavior of hers, boss didn't push for her promotion, which he was planning to do otherwise.

   It becomes even tougher to manage insecurities and expectations at work, as emotional reactions have very little acceptance at workplace.

4. **Fear of unknown**

   When things are ambiguous, and our brain doesn't get closure, another phenomena (DDG - which will be discussed later in the book) starts working.

   Non-closure, indefinite answers, ambiguous situations or abrupt decisions from others, create a fear of unknown in our brain.

   When we are not able to bring things to closure, the expectation automatically starts to increase from others to provide us a closure.

Remember, one of the primary function of our brain is to solve problems, however, if we are not able to get answers, it keeps working overtime to get the solution and get into an endless loop.

Example, I was working for this MNC, which announced its acquisition by another giant organization. The news gave a serious blow to lot others. In times of mergers and acquisitions, the biggest threat that people have is job redundancy. People started having insecurities and ambiguity about their roles, their brain started operating out of insecurities.

I became part of the team driving change management, and we could see how teaching people to deal with ambiguities helped.

The catch here is to command our brain to be OK with non-closures. Train the brain to wait for the right time, and take it one day at a time.

5. **Low-self esteem**

If you feel that you are powerless and helpless, you play a role of a VICTIM. Every victim needs a rescuer.

The rescuer in your life will unfortunately bear the load of your expectations. It can be extremely draining for the rescuer to keep fulfilling victim's expectations and hence after some time these kinds of relationships suffer a lot.

6. **Too much pampering in childhood**

If you are the one who received most of the stuff easily in life, the lucky one who had all the amenities and people standing with you whenever you needed them, then it is natural for child to assume that the world is great, and we get everything in platter from the people we love.

Problem comes, when we grow up and realize that not everybody in life is fulfilling our expectations.

These days in a bid to give a perfect life to our kids, given the resources that we have, we naturally aim to provide the best to our child so that he/she doesn't suffer, but unfortunately, that severely damages the emotional resilience of our children. It is important to put your foot down for somethings early in their lives, so they know they can't get everything that they want/need. Let them also work or struggle a bit to get stuff.

I never understood this thing earlier. Why would I want my daughter to go through pain, when I know it hurts? Let her be happy till the time she is with us, and I'm sure she will grow up to be a matured young lady and she will know how to manage stuff.

I realized the importance of this concept with one story, that deeply moved me. I still struggle a bit to follow my learning from this one but am much better now in putting my foot down and let her cry for some-time. It's hard!

Story: What happened to the butterfly?

Many of us know that a beautiful and colourful butterfly comes from an unappealing worm! Here is the story of a butterfly that was never able to live its life as a normal butterfly.

One day, a man saw a cocoon. He loved butterflies and had a craze for its wonderful combination of colours. In fact, he used to spend a lot of time around butterflies. He knew how a butterfly would struggle to transform from an ugly caterpillar into a beautiful one.

He saw the cocoon with a tiny opening. It meant that the butterfly was trying to make its way out to enjoy the world. He decided to watch how the butterfly would come out of the cocoon. He was watching the butterfly struggling to break the shell for several hours. He spent almost more than 10 hours with the cocoon and the butterfly. The butterfly had been struggling very hard for hours to come out through the tiny opening. Unfortunately, even after continuous attempts for several hours, there was no progress. It seemed that the butterfly had tried its best and could not give any more try.

The man, who had a passion and love for butterflies, decided to help the butterfly. He got a pair of scissors and tweaked the cocoon to make larger opening for the butterfly and removed the remaining cocoon. The butterfly emerged without any struggle!

Unfortunately, the butterfly looked no longer beautiful and had a swollen body with small and withered wings.

The man was happy that he had made the butterfly come out of the cocoon without any more struggles. He continued to watch the butterfly and was quite eager to see it fly with its beautiful wings. He thought that at any time, the butterfly might expand its wings, shrink the body and the wings could support the body. Unfortunately, neither did the wings expand nor the swollen body reduce.

Unfortunately, the butterfly just crawled around with withered wings and a huge body. It was never able to fly. Although the man did it with a good intention, he did not know that only by going through struggles the butterfly can emerge to be beautiful, with strong wings.

The continuous effort from the butterfly to come out of its cocoon would let the fluid stored in the body be converted into wings. Thus, the body would become lighter and smaller, and the wings would be beautiful and large. Struggles make us shine!

I connect a lot with this man, and his love for butterflies. So decided to let my child go through some struggle and sort it out on her own. I no more feel as much pain, when she is struggling, as I know each struggle will make her stronger.

Too much pampering in childhood, attempt from parents to preserve their children from pain, struggles and challenges, actually can lead to our high expectations of these children from others too, which in turn become a major factor of disappointment in life.

Tools to Reduce Our Expectations from Others

Tool 4: Challenge to Live by Yourself

Contradictory to what name suggests, this tool really helps in mending relationships.

If you are able to live and enjoy your time alone, here are the following things that you will experience –

1. More confidence
2. Better self-esteem
3. A strange sense of independence
4. A great sense of security
5. Time for reflections

These feelings, give our expectations from others some rest and help us reflect about life from different and larger perspectives.

It could be a big challenge in the beginning, as you might not know what to do, how to sit idle, or how to feel good about being alone and not with your loved ones. My advice is to just stay put, you'll start enjoying this new freedom gradually. As you accept it, you'll start getting ideas about how to enjoy this time. Join some classes, pursue a hobby, go for walks alone, experiment and explore stuff.

It's a change for people around you as well, so this might be a little difficult for them to digest in the beginning, that you are creating one part of life where they don't exist. It can bring up emotions in different ways, but remember your original intent is to bring more harmony and happiness in those relationships. Explain them, communicate your intent as many times as they want you to repeat. Stand for yourself, as remaining in the status quo, will only bring more vulnerability and self-esteem issues in your life.

Tool 5: Stay around Positivity: Be It People, Apps and Social Media

This tool is helpful in every way. Positive people who are generally happy, radiate positive energy. With them around, you will automatically feel empowered to be more independent. Join meet ups, Facebook communities and watsapp groups where positive subjects are discussed and shared. They are tremendously useful to change your state over a period of time.

Tool 6: Learn and Share At-Least One New Thing Every Day

This way your brain will have something positive to work on, and will not pay heed and attention to insecurities, fears etc.

Remember, the more positive learning, hobbies, and independence you add to your personality, the better will you fare in your relationships. This way, you will not be completely dependent on other people for your happiness and hence won't expect unrealistically from them.

I remember in the initial days of my married life, I realized that my husband had a great life, he had set of close friends with whom he wanted time off, he would plan his office parties and trips without any guilt of leaving me behind. I used to sulk and feel so horrible, I had no idea what to do. *I expected him to be with me all the time, I should have been his natural center of life like he is to me.*

The problem I identified later was, that me being a new wife had this programming in my mind that my husband is my life and everything that I do, needs to be around him. There is no one as important as him, not even me myself!

He would hate the fact that I use to sulk, and ask me to make new friends, go out and enjoy, but that use to hurt me even more.

It wasn't about him going out and enjoying that was hurting me, it was about ME being alone at home getting bored with nothing to look forward to, that was troubling me.

The moment I realized this, I made conscious efforts to go out with new people. I used to feel terribly bored and missed him around in the beginning, but as time passed by, I started enjoying doing certain things alone – like reading, attending hobby classes, coaching people. Guess what, I discovered my passion too in this process.

Here's the twist, as I was becoming independent and started enjoying my own company, he did face issues, he did miss me and honestly, I liked that, I did have some initial cheap thrills 😊, but then we had a deep talk, yes it boiled down to "his turn to figure out his passion." I'm thankful to him to push me out and explore myself, my identity, my passion. Remember that cocoon story!

Tool 7: Contracting

Sometimes people say that "we shouldn't expect from others," but it's as unrealistic as it can be. Yes, we shouldn't, but we do!

There are a lot of things we shouldn't do, but most of us haven't arrived that stage when we can truly live without expectations.

If you feel you are part of that group, where you understand that having expectations do hurt and we shouldn't, but it's not practically possible to implement it right now in some relationships, then this could be a great tool to reduce the mutual expectation pressure in any kind of relationship.

> "Contracting is a process in which people proactively think about what could possibly go wrong in this relationship, and they agree on some common way to resolve it in the most conducive and non-abrasive manner."

Examples of kind of verbal agreement on working styles help a boss-subordinate relationship:

1. I'm generally more active and responsive on mails after 12pm; before that sms/watsapp will work great
2. In case you disagree with any of my actions, give me feedback in person instead of in public
3. I'm ok working extra hours, however, there will be times when I might come late owing to my home commitments, hope you are ok with that.
4. I wish we connect at-least once in a week even if there's nothing important to discuss.

These contracts help in building trust-based relationships, as people get to know each other's challenges and expectations.

"Contracting is done over a period of time and it's not a formal process. It is always done before or after something goes wrong. It's not a good idea to start contracting when emotions are high."

It happens over a coffee, or any informal forum where you start this discussion about working styles. Pay more attention to what other people are expecting from you and then set your own expectations. *It's a mutual exercise and not a one-way practice.*

3. Other People's Expectations from Us

Life can be even more tough, if people start expecting a lot from us. Managing other people's expectations from us can be emotionally very draining.

The expectations of others keep increasing, as we continue to fulfill them. There is nothing wrong in fulfilling other people's expectations, in fact it's an important aspect of winning relationships.

However, if you feel drained out or find yourself to be a victim in the process of fulfilling other people's expectations, then it's time to do something about it.

Why People Expect from Us?

Largely people expect from us because of the following reasons –

1. They themselves do a lot of stuff for us
2. We haven't set clear expectations or contracting
3. Our own inability to say "NO"
4. They feel we have resources to help them
5. They are in the victim trap/mindset, and are feeling helpless
6. They aren't able to think through some innovative solutions to help themselves
7. To show others that you are close to them
8. They have their own insecurities and fears
9. We have been always helping them out
10. They feel that we will succumb to their grief and won't be able to say NO

Tools to Manage Other People's Expectations

Let's take a closer look at some of the tools to manage expectations that people have from us, without consciously hurting anyone's feeling.

Tool 8: Can You Sustain It, and Be Happy about It?

In a relationship that you want to last longer, ensure that you commit to doing things only if you can sustain the practice long term, else communicate honestly that it's just a one-time effort, and you won't be able to sustain it.

It's like this, I like working on presentations, but if my boss gives me a task to put excel reports together for him/her for 50% of my work time, and expects me to do it as part of my job, then it is important that I communicate my apprehension, rather than putting up with something that will drain me out.

One of my friends told me:

"I got married in a Rajasthan based family, and they still had a sort of Parda system despite living in an urban city, I was expected to cover my head at home, even while doing my daily chores if elders were around. I was extremely uncomfortable and knew for sure that I won't be able to sustain it. I had a heart to heart conversation with my mom-in law and put my foot down. We agreed that whenever her natives from village would come, I'll follow it, but rest of the times I can take it off! Phew!"

It is important to put your point of view across and discuss a mutually agreed solution, rather than succumbing to do things you don't like.

The key here is, do stuff with your 100% involvement and happiness. If you are doing it, be happy and ok about it, else it will add the stress level in your relationships.

Tool 9: Prioritize Your Relationship Circles

A bitter fact that remains constant in everyone's life is that almost everyone we know will have some or the other expectation from us and we can't keep everyone happy.

So how do we decide where to go that extra mile to fulfil someone's expectations. Make 4 concentric circles.

- Put yourself as the core of a circle
- Identify maximum 5–6 people who mean a lot to you, and put them in the inner circle
- Then put the next 10–12 people in the mid circle
- Rest in the outer circle

Now example, your boss comes in your inner circle at office, while your client comes in the mid-circle, then you know who to work with your boss closely and consult him in case of any unforeseen challenge.

Managing Expectations

In case both are in the inner circle, then it's best to get all of them together to find a solution.

Exceptions exist, when things go against your value system, and you are forced to make those difficult decisions, but we are keeping those extremes out of scope right now.

Tool 10: Keep Yourself at the Top and Take Sole Ownership for Your Decisions. Be the Hero, Not the Victim

It is important to take a decision basis the logic that appeals to you at that time, and then stand by it.

This is about me running my life, doing what I consider important. If you can live this tagline, people will start knowing you for this, and the expectations will automatically drop.

Extremely helpful when there's a conflict within people's expectations in your inner circle.

Keeping your own priority on top is important here. If you start feeling a victim in this situation, world will treat you like that and make you feel guiltier!

For example, my career, husband and my daughter all are important for my true happiness and form the inner circle.

There are times when I need to go for an urgent meeting, leaving her with grandparents. In this case, instead of feeling like a victim, I take a decision to go for the meeting, and still choose to be a HERO.

Because I feel like a hero - who is empowered enough, my daughter also finds it normal for me to go to office. She bids goodbye happily and then greets me with enthusiasm & pride when I'm back.

In case, she is sick, I take a decision to leave everything urgent and be with her. That's also my decision and if I have to face a brunt from office, so be it. I take full responsibility.

There was also a time, when I had my passion, job, home and kid to manage, I chose to quit regular job with equal grace.

End of the day it's a choice we are making keeping our own happiness in mind. The key is to not regret a decision you made for yourself. For if you are happy, others who love you will be happy.

People will also know that you will help only if that makes you happy, and you can't be taken for granted.

> "It is important to be a little selfish, to keep close ones happy."

Tool 11: Limit the Number of "Should(s) in Life; Replace with What You Want.

The herd mentality and auto-pilot are usually tied to the word "should." These come from our heads, our superego, the parent voice in our heads. Should(s) are by definition expectations imposed by others. When we fail to do them we feel guilty.

When we do follow them we often feel driven and expect a payoff for our efforts: *Since I am doing what I really don't want to do, I do expect others to appreciate, notice, give me a reward, pat me on the head, do what I expect.*

When the expected payoff doesn't come, our disappointment and resentment are fueled.

One of the ways, again to get away from should(s) in life is to focus on "What you want."

The expectations from others lower down considerably, when we do things that we want, instead of things that we should do, and we might not necessarily want to do.

Example: If you are not married, people expect you should get married, if you are married, then it is expected that you should have a child, if you have your child, then it is expected that you should have a second one.... People will keep putting the SHOULDs in your life till the time, you decide to stand up for yourself and decide what do you want and announce it clearly to the world.

Tool 12: Take Favors and Gifts from People Only If You Have the Intention and Status to Give Back, When Time Comes

I remember, in front of our house was a beautiful villa, very rich people, and they had a daughter, 3–4 years younger to me. We became good friends, and their parents started liking me a lot.

My visits to her home increased, and she also use to come to my house occasionally.

After a few days, my dad started acting weird, he started saying "NO" to certain things that I really didn't want to refuse. Examples –

1. My friend's mom said, I should start coming to their place every-day and give her tuitions and she will pay me. Given our financial pressures, I truly wanted to say yes! But my dad said NO and asked me to tell her that – she

Managing Expectations

       can come to my place anytime to study and I'd love to help her, but no money involved.

2. Her mom sent a beautiful jewelry piece that they bought specially for me during their vacation at Singapore! Can you imagine my excitement, but my dad said "NO" and got me to return it!

These were his words, and my lessons -

> **"When you make friends, accept things only when you can give in return.**
>
> **Do good for them without expecting anything in any form."**

These lessons do help keeping expectations at bay, be more giving, and set right expectations by accepting stuff only when we know we can return it with equal or more capacity.

4. Our Expectations from Life/Destiny

Have you heard these statements ever?

"Life has been very unfair to me"

"Don't know what destiny has in store"

"Even if I work hard, my destiny is bad and won't give me success"

"I have to work really very hard, to get what I want in life"

"Life is always tough for me"

"This shouldn't have happened to me"

"Why this happens to me all the time?"

If you've heard these statements, you know what I'm talking about.

A million-dollar truth is that **we don't know the future!**

At the max, we can only dream and work towards a goal. Whether we get it or not, whether we feel disappointed, or fail, is not in our hands. The sooner one accepts it, the better life gets.

In the event, life brings some unpleasant surprises here are few tools you can use to feel better.

Tools to Manage Your Own Expectations from Life

Tool 13: Take Your Learning and Let Go

Everything in life happens for us to take some learning, unless we don't learn from it, similar stuff keeps happening again and again.

It is important to reflect and internalize your learnings – this helps your life to look ahead and move forward.

Go back to the unpleasant incidents that continue to happen with you. Spend some time to reflect on what have been your learnings, what is it that you want to change when next time it happens.

Tool 14: Spend Your Time on Things That You Can Control or Influence

Stephen covey's book (7 habits of highly effective people) explains this concept beautifully, and I've lived this from last 10 years.

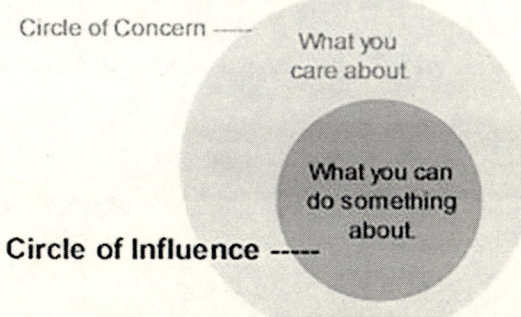

Figure 1.1 Circle of concern & Circle of influence

Managing Expectations

Highly effective and happy/satisfied people across the world spend +90% of their time on things that they can influence or control.

As their circle of influence increases, the circle of concern decreases automatically.

That is a proactive way of living life. Spend time wisely on things that you can do something about, instead of brooding over things that are not in your hands.

Example: Despite all my efforts, I'm not getting promotion or hike. What can I do about it? Either sit or crib or have a direct talk and take appropriate action. It's a Choice!

Tool 15: Let Go: Regrets and Guilt

Most of the people have some or the other reason to regret things and/or have guilt in life. They often blame the circumstances, and themselves or even others for not being able to handle stuff.

This is counterproductive for everyone in the eco-system. Being "OK" with it is the key.

It is a winning factor for the brain to keep you into negative and insecure zone, because intuitively people are more careful and guarded in that zone.

Whenever your brain tries to push you into the victim or the villain zone by reminding you of certain events that you regret or have guilt, here's what you can reprogram it to:

- I AM OK with whatever happened, I choose to move ahead
- Everyone makes the best choice available to them, in a given circumstance
- I forgive myself and choose to move ahead
- I take my learning from this, and choose to move ahead in life

Cursing life/destiny for things that you can't control is the biggest time waster and energy sucker act in life. Even if you don't, but your friend is doing it in front of you, immediately detach yourself from what he/she is saying. Or better still, change the topic!

There are two mental frames that everyone can operate from:

1. **Blame frame**: Where we keep cribbing about what's not working for us, what all went wrong in life, why we are not happy, how everyone is taking advantage of us, how things never work out!

2. **Outcome frame**: Where we shift from blaming to outcome. Key question we ask is – What can I do about it? How do I resolve or influence this situation?

The default mode of a human brain is go into blame frame, however, you can always program it to get into outcome frame when you feel you really are feeling drained with the former.

Going forward be conscious about the frame you are operating with. Blame frame can bring negativity, frustration, helplessness, while Outcome frame brings you the realistic approach to solution, hope, positivity.

Summary | Chapter 10

It is important for us to know that having expectations is a normal trait that all human beings have.

What is different between winners and losers is how you let those expectations impact you within yourself.

The chapter talks about 4 types of expectations, the possible root causes, and 15 tools to manage expectations.

Readers Reflections

1. There are different ways in which people express their love and affection, some by giving gifts, some by helping out, some by touch and others by telling you explicitly or giving you dedicated time. (Refer The 5 love languages). Just notice their behavior and determine the extent of love they are showering at you, you will be pleasantly surprised!

2. Expectations from others is always a result of some unfulfilled void inside, that we expect others or ourselves to fill in. The best way to keep away from this loop is to develop a capability to enjoy your time with yourself. Find out something that you can do and enjoy for hours. This soul cleansing action fulfils that void to a great extent.

11

Perceptions & Conflicts

"There are things that are known, there are things that are unknown, and in between are the doors of perception."

– Aldous Huxley

Simply defined, "Perception" is the way in which something is regarded, understood, or interpreted.

Perceptions play a huge role in our behavior, and therefore impact all kinds of relationships.

Most of the times, both parties in an argument are right from where they are looking at the situation.

Because of our varied cultures, backgrounds and experiences, we develop our own perception about things.

Perceptions & Conflicts

As shared in the picture above, most of the conflicts in our relationships at home or work arise owing to different perceptions of people.

A real-life example:

- You think your manager gives important projects to the same set of people, he should test others too
- Your manager thinks – he gives important and high visibility projects to people who voluntarily ask for it and are willing to go that extra mile

It's just the perception that is different, intent is not bad from both the ends. All it takes are few more steps to convert this conflict into a potential long-term partnership.

In this chapter, you will understand few tools to deal with conflicts that arise owing to difference in opinions/perceptions.

Tool 1: Respect Other Person's Perspective

This sounds like a simple tool but is often hard to follow owing to prevailing ego.

Normally, in case there is a conflicting point of view/perception, our ego works as a deterrent and there is an inherent need to win that make us argue and get into a conflict with the person in question.

These endless discussions become very draining as there comes a deadlock of perceptions.

A mature way to handle these deadlocks without losing your own point of view is to **Agree to Disagree.**

This way while you lose out in influencing or convincing the other person, but you emerge as a winner as a human, who respects individuality.

You will be surprised that the moment you use one of the phrases below, the person might agree with you too.

1. I understand your point of view, and here's my point of view about it, let's agree to disagree here
2. We have both experienced this same thing differently, hence may be there's no end to this discussion. Let's agree to disagree
3. Maybe both of us are stuck with our own individual experiences, I respect your point of view, let's agree to disagree

This tool is most useful when you are stuck in an argument, and you intuitively know that there's no end to it.

Tool 2: Perceptual Positions

This is a NLP (Neuro-Linguistic Programming) tool that you can utilize when you are alone.

There are times when we undergo extreme emotions owing to a conflict. Due to these overflowing emotions, it becomes very difficult to look at the situation or the person neutrally. Here's a great way to dissociate yourself.

P.S.: This tool involves a physical movement and might not work if you are doing all of this sitting or standing on one place.

Here's what you can do –

1. Identify 4 spots in the room that are visible to you, place a central spot where you can imagine the situation/event is happening

2. Physically move to the 1st position and look at the conflict situation (central spot), what is your point of view, your perception, why you are hurt, deliberate upon your emotions a bit. Once done, break your state by giving yourself a body shake. Take a deep breath and then physically move to the 2nd position.

3. In the 2nd position, assume the role of the person with whom you are having the conflict with. What is he/she thinking, his/her point of view, ensure that you concentrate and focus on playing the person's part and think like him/her. Once done, again break your mental state, shake your body a bit (clap or any stationary physical movement), take a deep breath, and physically move to the 3rd position.

4. In the 3rd position, assume the role of a person who is neutral and knows both of you. Look at both the previous positions and think about the situation from this neutral person's point of view. Once done, break your sate, take a deep breath and now move out of the 3rd position.

5. At a distance from all these 3 spots, choose a 4th position, from where you can look at all the 3. This position is of the supreme power/angel/god/mentor or anyone who you pay your highest regard. Carefully listen to what he/she is trying to tell you.

Once done, reflect what new insights you have about this situation. Has it changed a bit, were you able to experience detachment from a situation and looking at it from different angles?

If yes! Great! The more you use this tool, the better you get at it.

Perceptions & Conflicts

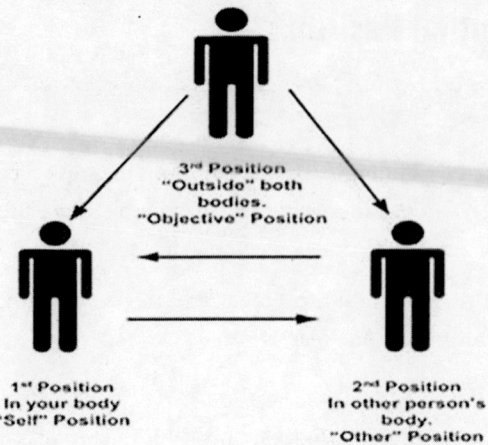

Additional tips about this tool:

1. In the beginning, to practice and experience this tool, choose a mild scenario which involves comparatively less emotions from your side.

2. There are times when we are so conscious and emotional that we are not able to think from other person's point of view, it's ok, you can move ahead to other positions and experience it.

3. Sometimes it becomes difficult to dissociate, it's ok, use some other tool, this tool works best for people who are more kinesthetic.

4. When you move into a different position, you need to assume the role of the other person, as if you are THAT another person.

Tool 3: Choose the Neutral & Positive Person to Talk It Out

I'm sure we have done this a lot of times, but remember, choose this neutral person very carefully. Choosing a wrong person to talk, can sometimes further complicates your situation.

There was a time when I was unhappy about petty things in life and I had a friend with whom I was extremely comfortable. I started sharing my disappointments with other people with her.

In her reaction, she would add on to my misery by proving how I was right in thinking that way, she would ask more questions that use to give me more reasons to crib. Things started getting worse.

I realized that talking to this neutral person who is not directly involved in my situation is not working out.

My suggestion is, choose a person who is positive and who will get you out of your negativity. Surround yourself with such people as much as you can.

In my case, I honestly spoke to my friend and did contracting that whenever I speak to you about something I'm unhappy about, I expect you to listen, but not acknowledge and add to the fire within me.

Luckily, she got the point and now we share stuff, but know when to stop and think positively, we know how not to add to the misery of each other.

Tool 4: Be Open to Understand Other's Perspective

This is one of the best ways to resolve a conflict or a difference of opinion.

> "The moment, you feel someone has said something that you don't agree with, instead of nodding your head big time to say NO, or pulling up the disagreement in your body language, get more *Curious* about it."

Ask questions like –

1. That's an interesting point of view, what makes you think like that?
2. Do you have any data or real experience to share
3. Help me understand this point better
4. Do you think, another point of view can also work here?

There is an immense power in the right questions. They not only help you understand other person's point of view, but also makes you look more mature as a person, who is not close to ideas.

Even better would be to admit in case you agree and tell the person, how his perception has changed your way of thinking.

Let's look at an example to explain this better

One person was arguing that the prayer works wonders, I didn't believe in it at that time, so asked him – what makes you say so.

Perceptions & Conflicts

I was amazed to know his scientific explanation about going to religious places, effect of sounds/vibrations of our prayers on our body etc.

I immediately thanked him for changing my opinion. I always looked at prayers from an angle of time pass for those who don't have too much work and don't want to face negativities.

In my view, helping someone is the best substitute to prayers.

Not that I was wrong, I still believe that helping someone in need is another form of prayer, but this additional information from the person, helped me appreciate the ones who believe in the power of prayers.

Tool 5: Mental Stance

This tool is extremely helpful to proactively manage a potential conflict.

In this tool, if you know that you are going ahead for a discussion with someone or a group, which will get heated, then, mental stance about this person or a group, play a big role to help you proactively avoid the conflict that may arise.

> "Mental stance is the judgment that you make in advance about the intention of a particular person or a group."

Let's look at this example: You manage a team of 10 people, today you are required to give feedback to one of your team members about his coming late and arrogant attitude.

In the normal scenario, here are few natural mental stances that might get created automatically in your brain –

- Today I'll show him the mirror and tell him that this attitude won't work!
- It's totally in vein to tell him anything, but it's ok will tell him once more, after all he is a good performer.
- I know what he thinks of me, if he messes with me, I'm going to show him the mirror today!

Negative mental stances like above, will most often kill your noble intent to coach or provide feedback.

> **"Mental stance plays a big role to shape your body language and behaviors."**

Now that you are aware that our brain naturally makes us think negative, if we were to re-program these stances positively, here's how they will look like –

1. Let me understand his point of view a little more today, so I can help him better
2. I will not give up on him, to bring a transformation in him through my consistent efforts. This will be my biggest win as a manager
3. Here's my chance to make a positive difference in his life, so he remembers me always for good reason

These positive mental stances, give you a great body language, patience and guide you throughout the discussion to make it positive and fruitful.

> **"Next time when you go for any difficult conversation, ensure that you re-check your mental stance and re-frame it positively if required."**

Summary | Chapter 11

Perceptions are the way in which something is regarded, understood, or interpreted. Perceptions largely define our behaviors, decisions and therefore relationships

Most of the times, we get into arguments or conflicts because of the difference in perceptions.

Here are few tools that we discussed in the chapter to deal with conflicts, disagreements and arguments proactively, by reprogramming some concepts in our own minds.

Tool 1: **Respect other person's point of view/perception**

Tool 2: **Perceptual positions**

Tool 3: **Discuss your point of view with a completely neutral party to understand other person's point of view**

Tool 4: **Be open to understand other's perspective**

Tool 5: **Mental Stance**

The most important point is to remember, that world can have different perceptions about different things, and everyone might be right. As a matured person, respect everyone's point of view, *respecting doesn't mean you agree with them*. You can disagree, but still respect someone's point of view.

12

Love & Attachment

"He who has no attachments can really LOVE others, for his love is pure and divine."

– Lord Krishna

I've deliberately picked up this topic, as following these principals made some major shifts in my own life.

Given below are some differences between love and attachment, which if understood can drastically improve your relationships and health.

Love Is Selfless, Attachment Is Selfish

Personal life context: When you're in love, you focus on making the other person happy. You're always thinking of ways to make sure that your partner feels loved and fulfilled. You aren't keeping score, arguing over who helps more, or fighting over who is supposed to wash the dishes. You don't emotionally blackmail your partner, try to manipulate them, or seek to dominate the relationship.

When you're merely attached to someone, you're focused upon the ways in which they can make you happy. You become heavily dependent upon your partner and may even try to control him or her to avoid abandonment. Instead of confronting your own issues, you use your partner to improve your self-esteem and fill a void within you. You believe that they are responsible for your happiness and become frustrated and angry if they fail to bring you contentment.

Workplace context: Being an effective manager or team member will mean making contribution with a pure intent, so that the team is effective, organization's results are achieved.

Your actions will be in the best interest of the team and organization, without any manipulations, domination etc.

Love & Attachment

Some more examples to experience love at workplace are given below:

- If you feel someone can do better at a job than you, then you will happily go ahead with the decision.

- As a manager, if you feel you can't further grow a top performer, you give him chance to move into different teams where there are better growth prospects, instead of thinking selfishly about the short-term inconvenience to your team.

- With your clients, if you think a particular product is not suitable, despite the fact that it is costlier, you choose not to be selfish and manipulative, and give what makes sense. In case your organization gets upset about it -
    - ✓ Check the intent of the organization/manager
    - ✓ Share your intent and how you are thinking about long term brand image and relationships.

- It is better to live your values and love others for your own sake, so make an appropriate choice.

Love Is Liberating, Attachment Is Controlling

Personal context: Mutual love allows you to be your true self. Your partner encourages you to be who you genuinely are, and you won't be afraid to expose your weaknesses. Mutual trust develops and becomes a powerful catalyst for personal growth for both of you. Love is never controlling. In actuality, love transcends control. Your partner's ability to accept you for who you are and encourage you to pursue your dreams allows you to let go of the need to control their life.

Attachment, on the other hand, tends to fuel controlling behavior. You may discourage your partner from spending time with their friends, play mind games, or put an unhealthy level of focus on pleasing them. You may even try to manipulate them into staying with you regardless of their feelings.

Workplace context: You must have noticed that the word "Coaching" is taking over the process of "Feedback." The strategy of coaching is liberating, as it gives the freedom to the team member to choose the way he/she would like to go ahead and improve the performance.

Similarly, at work, you as a manager wouldn't want to control people using your powers, instead a better approach is whole heartedly accept their failures, and weaknesses till the time it doesn't hurt the collective output. If it does hurt, then instead of resorting to control, new age manager would bring his team together and collaborate for best results. Be more democratic, listen to them, respect feelings and instill inspiration and aspiration to do better. Pleasing team members/peers, or downplaying, manipulating them is never an option for a person who loves his workplace.

Love Is Mutual Growth, Attachment Is about "Falling down"

For both personal and work context: If you're in love, you and your team/partner will grow together. When both of you work to become the best versions of yourselves, you'll become better than you could have on your own. In short, your partner/team stimulates your growth, and you do the same for them.

In cases of attachment, your urge to control and your inability to solve your own problems restricts your growth as well as your partner's/team's growth. Your unresolved issues cause unnecessary dependence upon your team/partner. Not surprisingly, this restricts the growth of both parties and makes it difficult to love in a healthy way

Love Is Everlasting, Attachment Can Get Over

Personal context: Love survives the passage of time. You and your partner may ultimately breakup, be it temporarily or permanently. If you were truly in love, however, that person will always have a place in your heart and you will continue to wish them well for the rest of their life.

If, on the other hand, you were merely attached to them, you will likely hold resentment after a breakup. You may even experience feelings of betrayal. These feelings stem from the assumption that your partner had an obligation to make you happy, that in your eyes, was not fulfilled.

Workplace context: Even if you or your team members leave the organization, the relationship and contact remains. As you move up the ladder, your leadership quality is defined by the number of followers you have. Your connect and relationship with people even after separation in different organizations or teams defines your leadership.

I simply follow what my dad says – "no matter how much you fight with me, you are my children and I will still love you."

I experienced so much of liberation in this statement, that I worked very hard for few years to shed my ego, and be there for people unconditionally, even if we've had worst of fights, even if I never received any apology that I deserved, even if I was hurt or betrayed, I maintained this stance in me – no matter what you are my friend, you are my family, I will not stop loving you. Let's start again.

Now, there is a catch in unconditional long-lasting love feeling from your side. There is a possibility that the person from the other side is not mature enough and doesn't stop hurting or betraying you. My only advice here is – be smart (specially at work), keep your intentions good, and ensure that you are guarded with better strategies to avoid the same issues again.

Let me share one example to understand this better:

One of the john's team member, Satish, use to take a lot of unscheduled leaves, it was becoming very difficult for others at work to cope up with additional work pressure, so john decided to talk to him about it.

Satish was a bit arrogant initially and told him that he needed this flexibility owing to this part time MBA course that he just enrolled for. They did agree to an interim solution, so Satish could manage the course, but it didn't last long, and he again resorted to taking unscheduled leaves.

After repeated dialogues quite a few times, John had to take a decision to issue him a warning letter. It was in the organization's best interest. Finally, Satish was upset about the warning letter and left the job. John bid him a nice farewell and kept sending him best wishes months after months.

After around 2 years, Satish finally called up John and apologized for his behavior.

There was no need for Satish to do that, they were in different parts of the world and the incident had happened long time back.

But it happened, because John's intent was for the best interest of the organization and he took a rational decision, despite the fact that he loved Satish and his work.

Sometimes, it is easier we do get into dilemmas like these. Remember "love" doesn't mean you don't call spade a spade, or you don't argue with the other person. Love means, despite all the disagreements, you still forgive, forget and get back to normal routine without any grudges.

Experimenting this approach with few people to start with, all it needs is to just KILL your EGO to prove yourself right and keep doing your duty with utmost honesty.

No matter how much a mother loves her child, but it is important for her to take strict actions when the child resorts to misbehavior or some unpardonable act. It doesn't mean that she no more loves her child, it just means that she is gearing the child up for success and happiness in the long run.

Love Reduces Ego, Attachment Boosts Ego

When in love, you become less self-centered. Your relationship serves to reduce your ego, fosters your growth, and encourages you to become less selfish and more loving. The relationship you have with your partner fuels positive changes for both of you. More importantly, you'll both have the courage to share your weaknesses, expose your vulnerabilities, and communicate from the heart.

Alternatively, relationships based on attachment are typically dominated by the ego. This is why many people repeatedly fall into a continuous stream of unsatisfying relationships, each of which involves the same, recurrent problems. You find it difficult to look within and resolve your issues. This generates dependency within your relationship, which triggers the feeling that you can't be happy without your partner. You rely on your significant other to solve your problems or, at the very least, help you forget them.

Here are some common questions that people ask me during coaching sessions, regarding love and attachment –

What do I do, if I realize my mistake in a conflict, but now the person is angry or indifferent with me.

When I'm in love with someone and I realize that I committed a mistake which did hurt the other person, I will have no qualms to say sorry – even if it takes 1000 times.

At the same time, I will give time for the person to forgive me and get back. I won't expect the person to necessarily forgive me, I will respect his/her decision to come back or not.

If at all the person comes back, I will accept him/her whole heartedly with utmost respect. If the person decides to not come back, I'll choose to respect his/her decision and forgive myself at the same time.

Love doesn't need physical presence of the person with you, it's a feeling for someone that's there with you even if that person is not present.

So my feelings for the person will remain the same, and I'll pray that the person is happy wherever he/she is.

Does unconditional love mean giving rights to people to hurt us and we will not react?

In today's world, it is difficult for most of the people to keep bearing the hurt from a loved one.

So here's a quick answer to this question –

Above love for everyone else, you need to start loving yourself unconditionally. That's the first step to love others. If a relationship has gone to a level, where your self-esteem is getting hurt, you have all the rights to do what is right, move ahead, and still love and forgive that person.

Your moving on doesn't mean that you didn't love the person, your moving on from something only means, that you are protecting yourself. You have full rights to do that.

When it comes to children, is it by default the "Love" for them, or can it be "Attachment" too? How do we know?

Attachment comes with conditions. If you see yourself putting a lot of conditions in any relationship, like –

1. I won't talk to you if you marry that girl
2. I will leave you and go to old age home if you don't do this
3. You will not leave me alone here and go to abroad ever!

These statements suggest conditions in relationships, which are a testimony to attachment instead of love.

Yes, when a child is totally dependent on parents for basic needs and does everything under the sun to tire them out, if parents are still taking care, feeding and playing with him/her, that's definitely unconditional love!

Unconditional love at workplace? Are you serious? How?

The whole concept of unconditional love at workplace can be very tricky. One thing that helped me was, that my first priority for unconditional love is my organization, and then comes everyone else at work.

- This helps me take a stand when I think organization will not be benefitted from a particular decision
- It helps me take tough calls when I decide to let go of people, even when I like them as a person
- It helps me do things for the organization's benefit, even if I've to go that extra mile and stretch

Summary | Chapter 12

The words, Love and Attachment are often used interchangeably, however there is a big difference between the two. One leads to empowerment while other leads to miseries.

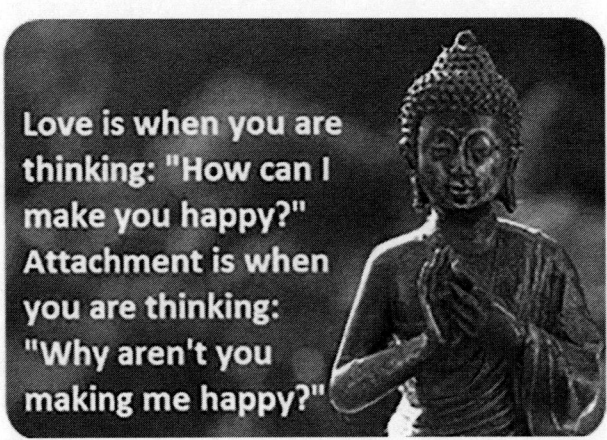

The chapter talks about 5 differences between love and attachment, that can help you identify your state in your relationships.

1. **Love is selfless, attachment is selfish**
2. **Love is liberating, attachment is controlling**
3. **Love is mutual growth, attachment is about "falling down"**
4. **Love is everlasting, attachment can get over**
5. **Love reduces ego, attachment boosts ego**

Reader Reflections

While reading this chapter, there will be times, when your brain will completely reject the ideas.

That's a sign of your attachment to the EGO... Attachment to "I."

Read this chapter again and again, specially at times when you are in a true learning state and your brain is ready to experiment with new approach.

Love & Attachment

- Think about a relationship that cause you a lot of pain.
- Do you have love or attachment or both with this person?
- What can you do today, to reduce the attachment that you feel for this person?
- What is that one condition that you can waive off in your relationship with this person?
- Start slow, one condition at a time, and you will see, you'll free up yourself with a lot of burden!

13

The Depth of "Communication"

The NLP Communication Model, developed by Tad James & Wyatt Woodsmall (1988) from the work of Richard Bandler & John Grinder (1975), is one of the key structures in Neuro-Linguistic Programming (NLP).

I have been teaching and learning about communication from since last 20+ years, however, this model resonated the most with me, and I could instantly feel the transformation within. That's the power of NLP tools.

I am picking up a simple yet awesome self-discovery tool which is part of NLP communication model. It's called DDG.

Before we move on to explain the model, read this case study, which will make it easier for you to understand.

Case Study

Mahesh had a terrible argument with Sundar- his boss, at work in front of the entire team. They often use to debate, but this one was way more heated than ever.

After around 20 minutes they decided to leave it half-way and go back to their desks.

The Depth of "Communication"

After that day, Mahesh didn't come to office for around a week. He didn't answer any calls from office. His peers were curious and enquired about him from the boss, Sundar, however there was no definitive answer. Discomfort could be clearly seen on Sundar's face when asked about Mahesh.

Discussions started happening during lunch and coffees about the confrontation the other day, and there was a grapevine that Mahesh was looking out for another job and was too upset about the discussion the other day.

After around a week, when Mahesh came back at work, he had a visible disengagement while doing his job. His peers could notice the change in his behavior and enquired him, to which he just answered casually.

The discussions on the lunch and coffee tables became more serious. The story was getting completed - how Mahesh must have felt so insulted the other day, that he took leave and then resigned over an e-mail, now he must be serving his notice period and that's why he looks so disengaged.

They also started talking about how important it is to keep in the good books of this boss else he will compel you to leave. They talked about how everyone must eventually follow the bosses and avoid conflicting discussions.

This went on for around 2 more weeks, both Sundar and Mahesh were not seen communicating much.

Suddenly one day, the team saw Sundar in a completely old avatar (style). He had a sweet box in his hand and offered it to the whole team. And this is when he told them the entire story: After going back from work that day, he got the news that his dad was suffering from a very serious kidney problem, and doctors had advised for an immediate transplant. While the kidney was luckily available, they decided to go for the surgery the same week, that's why he didn't come for the week. Sundar was a catalyst in his situation, where not only he gave leave and support to Mahesh but also helped him financially.

Mahesh had requested Sundar to not tell this to the team, till everything is over, as he didn't want to bother anyone and would have felt uncomfortable with the anticipated sympathetic behaviors and questions.

Today his dad was back home with great reports after the successful transplant, so he bought the sweet box!

Before moving into the analysis of this case study, let me first explain you the concept of DDG.

Introduction to D.D.G.

Negative, vague language can work for or against you. Whether self-talk or dialogue with others, generalizations we make, details we leave out, or the way we distort through language, greatly influence how we think, feel, and act.

You can **choose** *vague language* that can limit you or *artfully vague language patterns* that are positive and empowering.

Just be conscious about the language you use, and see the magic unveil.

Generalization

Generalization is where the speaker takes a particular experience applies it generically to a multitude of other situations (generalizes.)

Examples:

- One must dress up great, to get positive attention
- All children make a nuisance when left alone
- Nobody loves me
- It is not possible for a mother, to do a job and take good care of children at the same time

Words to listen for:

- Can't, unable, not possible.
- Need, must, have to, go to, necessary, requirement.
- Everybody, nobody, anyone, every, always, never.

Questions to ask:

- According to whom? Have you also seen normally dressed people getting positive attention? What makes you say that? How do you know?
- Need? Which children? Discipline in what way? What else do they need? who says?
- Nobody? Is there one person who doesn't? What tells you that? How are you measuring love? How do you love anyone?
- According to whom? Are there any good mothers you have seen who are managing both? Have you checked with other working moms? What data do you have to prove it? How do you define good care?

The Depth of "Communication"

Deletion

Deletion is where details are deleted as the speaker chooses what to focus on.

Examples

- He's a failure
- Her children are not very bright.
- She rejected me.
- They were left to fend for themselves.

Words to listen for:

- Instances where a verb has been turned into a noun such as 'failing at' become 'failure' or 'he is performing' becomes 'his performance' or 'he is succeeding' becomes 'his success.' These nouns sound like individual judgments.
- Those which require an opposite such as good, bad, cold, hot, bright, dull, insincere, happy, sad, rich, poor.
- Verbs which require clarification.
- Non-specific references to people/things such as they, people, computers, children.

Questions to ask:

- How did he fail exactly? What did he fail at? Who says so? Has he failed at everything he's done? Is there nothing he has succeeded at? Has he not succeeded at drawing your attention? What else is he succeeding with?
- Compared to whom? What standard/who are you measuring them against? Bright in what way?
- What did she do that you are calling rejection?

Distortion

Distortion is when the speaker distorts something to mean something it was not intended to mean.

Examples:

- He never buys me flowers, I don't think he loves me.
- My children are driving me crazy.

- I know you don't want to support my initiative.
- Families should stick together through all life's challenges.

Words to listen for:
- Statements that don't 'add up,' where a conclusion stated in the second part is based on the meaning attached in the first part.
- Statements in which one thing causes another.
- Statements which include conjecture and suggest mindreading – example: I know.
- Statements lacking reference to the author.

Questions to ask:
- In what way does him not buying you flowers mean that he doesn't love you? So what ways does he show that he loves you?
- What specifically are you doing that causes you to feel crazy? What are your children doing when you choose to go crazy?
- How do you know? What tells you that? Can you read my mind?
- According to whom? Who said that? Who are you quoting?

Case Study Analysis

Now that you have understood the concept of Generalization, Deletion and Distortion, and how we can counter the unproductive pattern of mind through questions, let's re-look at the case study shared earlier in the chapter.

Where do you think deletion occurred?

It occurred when Sundar didn't share with the team the reason why Mahesh is not coming. Of course, it was based on Mahesh's request.

What were the examples of distortions in the case study?

"When our mind doesn't get direct information that we need, it starts making assumptions to complete the story. This phenomenon is also called distortion."

Now, in the case study, when people didn't get a clear answer about where Mahesh was, they started putting all the incidents together and created a story that Mahesh and Sundar had a bad argument, Mahesh was upset and he must have resigned.

The Depth of "Communication"

Even after Mahesh was back at work, his changed behavior made them believe their theory and grapevine kept getting deeper.

Generalization in the Case Study

"When our story is complete in the mind, irrespective of the facts or assumptions, the natural next step is to draw a generic learning out of it."

That's generalization. Generalization can be made of facts or assumptions, they also sound like beliefs.

In the case study, when people completed their story based on assumptions, the other generalizations that came with it were –

- *It is always important to be in the good books of bosses, else they compel you to leave.*
- *Everyone must eventually follow the bosses and avoid conflicting discussions.*

With these deletions, distortions and generalizations that were created at the workplace, imagine the kind of brand this manager earned, the kind of culture and behaviors that prevailed, the kind of frustrations and reactions that people would have encountered.

Luckily in this case study, Mahesh came back and told the truth to everyone, however the generalizations have power to stay a little longer in mind if not questioned. These counter-productive generalizations later create a lot of issues in relationships.

Catch yourself red-handed when you are telling in your mind similar stuff like below:

1. He doesn't love me/respect me
2. This always happen to me
3. I can never get things done from anyone, I'm good doing it myself
4. I always feel depressed and lonely
5. Bosses should never be trusted, they are selfish and on the side of management

Summary | Chapter 13

In order to manage your emotions, reactions and triggers, it is important that you do this exercise and think carefully about the kind of generalizations, deletions and distortions you have created in your mind for a particular aspect of life.

Are they true, can they be verified, can you remove all the deletions? Ask tough questions and open these mental knots that deeply scar relationships at times.

Reader Reflections

- Can you recollect any 4 generalizations that you have regarding relationships (Personal or work?)
  - ✓ Write these down, and question them?
- Think about your previous conflicts and reflect if there was any information deletion or distortion that happened by either side.
- Remember, distortions seep in very easily in your brain, it is important that you keep a check and question yourself about why are you thinking that? Do you have facts or is it just an assumption that is temporarily making you feel better?
- If you think the person is deleting some information, seek more information, clarify your doubts to avoid distortions.

14

Emotional Vocabulary

In the world today, when artificial intelligence is taking over the natural human instincts, social media is taking over the in-person interaction time, when the attention spans are reducing to mere few minutes/seconds, a common and most obvious side effect that's affecting our species is **"stress from our own inability to deal with emotions."**

This challenge has aggravated so much in last few years, that "Emotional Intelligence" has taken the front seat in all social settings. People with high EI *(emotional intelligence)* are known to be the winners in every field. Only technical knowledge and other talent will not be able to take you to the top these days, **emotional intelligence** is a distinct skill that differentiates a person from good to great.

There is enough study and researches available on the internet for you to believe in this statement.

Here's one Emotional Intelligence tool that I'm going to share with all of you, that's extremely simple yet reaps amazing benefits, specially to build winning relationships.

Emotional Vocabulary

Defining the term "emotional vocabulary" is as simple as it sounds: associating words with our emotions.

How It Helps?

In our brain, emotions are produced in the limbic chamber, while there is a separate chamber for logical and rational thinking (neo-cortex) which also includes language processing.

When we are emotional, our limbic brain is active and produces lot of chemicals, while rational brain is all confused about what is happening, and sometimes fails to take over.

Emotional vocabulary plays a role of a bridge to activate the logical thinking chamber when we are emotional. Figure 1.2

The moment we are able to associate a word (language) to the emotion, our logical brain starts processing the word and by default gets activated. This helps us use our rational as well as emotional brain together. "Emotional Intelligence" is the ability to act in guidance of both emotional and rational brain. Emotional vocabulary makes it possible.

Emotional vocabulary helps us to regulate our emotions and engage in positive social interactions and responses.

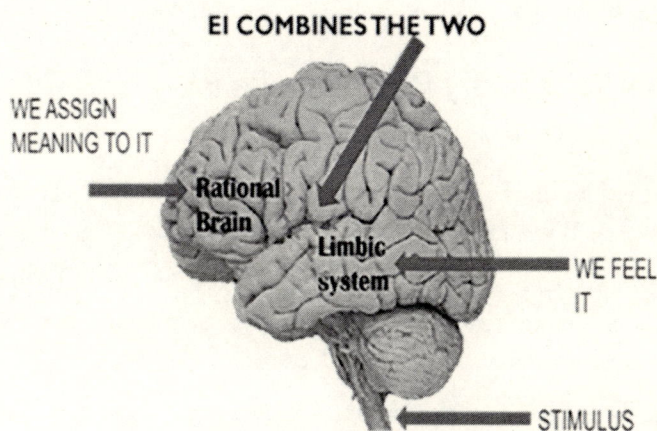

Figure 1.2 EI combines the rational and limbic brain

People who are emotionally intelligent are aware of how and what they are feeling most of the times.

In my emotional intelligence workshops, I ask people to describe emotions and challenge them to come up with as many words as they can. In a group of 25–30

Emotional Vocabulary

members, after really pushing their memory, together they come up with merely 65 – 70 words in total on an average.

Do you know, there are 600+ words in the diction to describe feelings and emotions?

The more words you remember and associate with, the better your EI score will become. Hence, the only simple task is, when next time you are feeling heavy with emotions, remember to identify the name of that emotion. You will see the magic happening itself.

This is one of the biggest habit to win relationships in the personal and professional life.

It is important to express your own feelings to self as well as others in all kinds of relationships.

No matter how much you say that feelings don't work in corporates – the fact remains – 'feelings' and 'how you manage/express them' is the only factor that differentiates successful leaders with unsuccessful ones.

With millennials working with us, EI has become even more important than ever before. If you are not able to connect with your millennial workforce at a feeling level, they are not going to work with you with full passion. Accept this hard truth and start with using just this simple tool.

The Emotional Vocabulary Reference Chart

Here's a quick glimpse of emotional vocabulary chart.

In Figure 1.3, the feelings in the outermost section are the words describing feelings with low intensity, and as you move inside the intensity increases.

The idea is to learn and use as many emotions described in this chart as possible. Awareness about your emotions will help you deal with them better. The problem occurs when we are not sure about what are we feeling.

If you look at the core, there are 6 basic most intense feelings: Anger, Fear, Surprise, Happy, Sad, Disgust. Rest all of them are the intensity variants of these 6 core feelings.

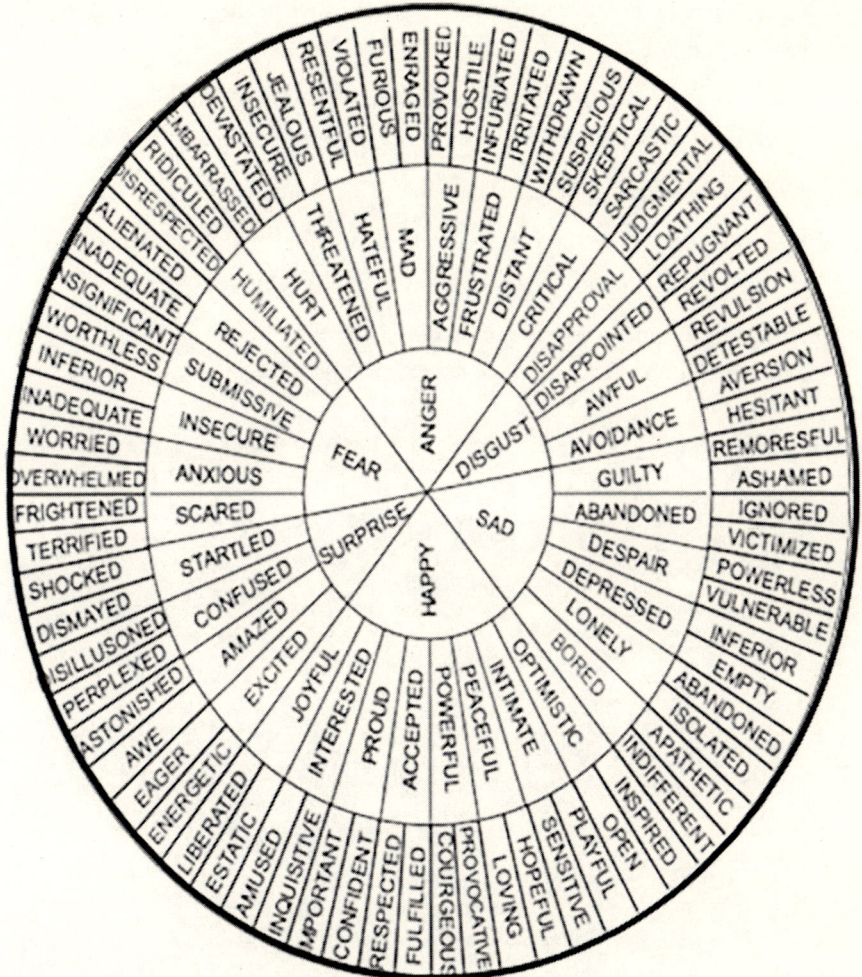

Figure 1.3 The emotional vocabulary chart

Different ways of using Emotional Vocabulary

- Daily before sleeping, refer to this list and write/recite at-least 3 emotions you went through during the day, a good exercise to do with family.

- Put this emotional vocabulary chart on your phone or any device that remains with you most of the times. Whenever you feel the gush of emotions, just look at this chart and associate the right feeling word that resonates with your emotion at that time. Notice the magic happening within you after that.

Emotional Vocabulary

- Help others to identify the name of the feeling when they come to share and vent out on you.

- Play the feeling dumb-charades at work or with children at home. It accentuates the emotional/rational brain along-with breaking the ice.

- Learn and internalize at least one new feeling word every day.

- Identify the top 5 feelings that you clearly identify in yourself when you go through them, and 5 that you've never been able to identify with.

- Many organizations provide these mood charts to be put on desks. Largely helps as an icebreaker or a topic for a small talk.

My Mood Today

Summary | Chapter 14

Emotional vocabulary is the simplest way to boost your self- awareness about your emotions.

There are 600+ words that describe emotions, if we identify the right word/language for our emotions, the logical brain comes into action and prevents us to react irrationally.

This is one of the best and most advisable knowledge we must provide to our children, so they grow up to become much more emotionally intelligent and resilient.

It helps reduce the intensity of emotions that we feel by activating the logical brain sooner than anything else.

Can be utilized in lot many ways, start simple and realize the magic happening within and outside you.

Reader Reflections

- Recall all the words that you know that describe emotions. Add 1 more word to your emotional vocabulary every-day.

- If someone is venting out or crying in front of you, just help them describe that emotion, using your vocabulary. This is applicable to anyone from a 3-year-old to adult of any age.

    Example, when my daughter is very angry and throwing tantrums for something, I immediately hug and ask her - tell me what you are feeling. She burst out – I'm MAD, I'm ANGRY… and after just a few seconds feel normal. The trick works almost every time. Sometimes I help her identify the word by saying – I understand you are feeling "XYZ…"

15

Gratitude List

"It is not happy people who are thankful, it is thankful people who are happy."

– Anonymous

In this chapter, we will cover the importance and impact of the word "thank you" – or "Gratitude." Why and how it creates magic inside and outside us. We will also discuss some tools to make our gratitude list super-charged, so it truly solves its purpose.

My 4 – year old daughter, got her holidays homework. While not many like homework, this one was quite creative and action oriented.

One task that caught my attention was about using the magic words and one of those was – "Thank you." While we think "Thank you" comes naturally to us as it's a habit cultivated from childhood, here's what I experienced from her holiday homework.

- I didn't thank my maid enough in words, I did give her money, clothes and gifts but never expressed in words. I don't know why. She stood by me and worked extra hours whenever required, and never made faces. If you are in India, you will understand the emotions behind it ☺.
    - ✓ When I did say it in as many words and told her why I was thankful, she was initially surprised and then couldn't stop her tears and hugged me! An emotion so pure, I hugged her tight and felt like a human
- I never thanked the cup of tea which made my day every morning! It sounded silly, but I tried and wow it was fun.
- I along-with my daughter started consciously thanking everything, her toys, our bed, our pillow, our house, the park, the people who helped us in simple ways. We shared laughter and the great feeling every-time we did that.
- I loved her innocent explanations about why we are thanking her "peppa pig" toy – because it makes her smile, everytime she plays with it,

thanking the pillow, because it provides her head a support and she gets a good sleep!

During this exercise, I had one thought - Can we ever thank enough?

The answer is "No," as a human being, we have so much to feel gratitude for, that we can never ever thank enough.

The key is – know the reason and tell the reason, why are you thanking something or someone! That reason if spoken makes a huge difference, if not spoken remains dormant in our mind and doesn't create as much impact.

But what impact are we talking about here? I reflected what's the difference and here are few things that not only I experienced, but there are billions of people out there who have acknowledged that they experienced.

Impact of Gratitude

Let me list down top 5 impacts of gratitude, while there is no doubt there are many more.

- **Gratitude increases our well being**

    A five-minute a day gratitude journal can increase our long-term well-being by more than 10 percent. That's the same impact as doubling your income!

- **Gratitude makes people like us**

    Gratitude generates social capital – in two studies with 243 total participants, those who were 10% more grateful than average had 17.5% more social capital.

    Gratitude makes us nicer, more trusting, more social, and more appreciative. As a result, it helps us make more friends, deepen our existing relationships, and improve our marriage.

- **Gratitude boosts our career**

    Gratitude makes you a more effective manager, helps you network, increases your decision-making capabilities, increases your productivity, and helps you get mentors. As a result, gratitude helps you achieve your career goals, as well as making your workplace a more friendly and enjoyable place to be.

Gratitude List

- **Gratitude makes us healthier**

RESULTS	STUDY	DATE
Keeping a gratitude journal caused participants to report - 16% fewer physical symptoms, - 19% more time spent exercising - 10% less physical pain - 8% more sleep, and - 25% increased sleep quality	Counting Blessings Versus Burdens	2003
The emotions of appreciation and gratitude shown to **induce the relaxation response**	The grateful heart	2004
A gratitude **visit reduced depressive symptoms** by 35% for several weeks; A gratitude **journal lowered depressive symptoms** by 30%+ for as long as the practice was continued	Positive Psychology Progress	2005
Patients with hypertension were instructed to count their blessings once a week. There was a significant **decrease in their systolic blood pressure**	Gratitude: Effects on perspectives and blood pressure	2007
Gratitude correlated with **improved sleep quality** (r=.29), **less time required to fall asleep** (r=.20), and **increased sleep duration** (r=.14).	Gratitude Influences sleep through the mechanism of pre-sleep cognitions	2009
Levels of gratitude significantly **correlated with vitality and energy**	Multiple studies	Many

There are enough studies and reasons to believe gratitude can extend your lifespan by a few months or even years.

- **Gratitude strengthens our emotions**

    Gratitude reduces feelings of envy, makes our memories happier, lets us experience good feelings, and helps us bounce back from stress. Gratitude also plays a big role in shedding our ego.

Supercharge Your Gratitude List

"When you are grateful, fear disappears and abundance appears."

– **Anthony Robbins**

While making a gratitude list is not too much of a task, it's as simple as writing or typing down on your favorite device about things and people you are most grateful for.

However, the catch here is that

> "Gratitude list is not merely a tick in the box work. If you don't feel the emotions associated with it, writing them won't make any difference."

Given below are some ways in which you can supercharge your gratitude list –

- Make it colorful, add pictures, drawings or your mental maps.
- Detail it out using words that describe your feelings for that thing, people or event.
- Provide reasons as to why you are grateful for a particular person, thing or event? Wherever possible, supercharge it by telling these reasons to the person directly.
- Saying that I love my mom and am thankful for having her in my life – might not work as well as stating reasons as to why you are thankful for her to be part of your life.

Here's an example –

- I am so thankful to have my mom in my life because
    - ✓ Her long tight hugs make me feel very secured
    - ✓ Her presence makes me feel like a child
    - ✓ I always have one person who doesn't judge me, no matter whatever I do and confess to her
    - ✓ She enjoys my happiness and makes me feel special by cooking my favorite dishes
    - ✓ She brings smile to me with her innocent questions about technology and comments about the games on phone that she never wins 😊

Once you have supercharged your list, remember to read it often, at-least once a day to start with, and especially when you feel low.

You will notice that this habit of creating your gratitude list will make you feel very elated, reduces the ego and stress considerably from your life. You will start enjoying your relationships even more.

If you're not thankful for what you have, why should you get anything more?

– Anonymous

Summary | Chapter 15

The act of gratitude is by far one of the simplest ways to improve the quality of life and happiness quotient of our lives.

There are many studies that have proven that the habit of gratitude not only impacts our health and increases the life span, but also have a huge impact on our emotional well-being and relationships.

The only catch is to ensure that gratitude list is made with all the emotions that you feel. It shouldn't be just another task on your checklist.

The emotions can be generated for a gratitude list, by detailing it out, adding more visuals, confessing it to the people directly etc.

Absence of gratitude, increases the ego in our system and brings a whole lot of miseries and stress in our lives. Relationships suffer big time if gratitude for them is not enough thought and expressed.

16

Affirmations

> Convince the subconscious that you are what you want to be.
>
> This is affirmation. Repetition of affirmation leads to belief, and when belief becomes conviction things begin to happen!

While the concept of affirmations has been hugely popular over the last few years, Louis Hay being the mother of the concept.

In this chapter I will share how it helps, why it works and also some of the sample affirmations lists for your immediate relationship challenges.

I was introduced to affirmations by a very close friend Snehal Kamath, when I was in tremendous fear and pressure. Can never thank her and Louise Hay enough☺

What Are Affirmations?

As per Louis Hay, every thought you think and every word you speak is an affirmation. All of our self-talk, our internal dialogue, is a stream of affirmations. You are using affirmations every moment whether you know it or not. You are affirming and creating your life experiences with every word and thought.

As a certified NLP (Neuro-linguistic Programming) Master practitioner, coach and facilitator, I understand *affirmations as a brain re-programming tool.*

Our thought patterns are by default set to negative and critical by our brain. It's only now, when the world is waking up to "Thoughts create experiences" formula, people are moving towards positivity, yoga, meditation etc. These elements have never caught so much attention so far. As they say, the SECRET is out.

Affirmations

In order to change this default programming into a winning positive mode, we need to start feeding positive thoughts with right language into the brain.

The sentences framed with positive thoughts with right language are called "Positive Affirmations." These are specially designed to instruct our brain to change our thinking pattern.

How & Why It Works?

We all have in our brains a thing called a Reticular Activating System (RAS), which is like a filter that lets in information that we need and filters out the information that we don't. If we didn't have this system, we would be bombarded with so much information that our senses would overload, and we would go into massive overwhelm. Instead, our brain registers what matters to us based on our goals, needs, interests, and desires.

For example, when me and my husband decided to finally have a child, we invariably noticed more number of maternity clinics & hospitals on the same road we traveled for last so many years, TV channels seemed to have subscribed more baby advertisements, pregnant ladies were all around us – in shopping malls, restaurants, office etc. as if this was an exclusive baby boomer era.

When you say an affirmation over and over again, a couple of things happen.

One is that it sends a very clear message to your RAS that this is important to you. When you do that, brain gets busy noticing ways to help you achieve your goals.

If ideal weight is your emphasis, you will suddenly begin to see every gym and weight loss product. If money is your goal, investment and earning opportunities will move to the forefront of your awareness. In essence, the affirmation can kick your creativity into high gear.

You are so much in sync with what you want using affirmations, that you almost forget all the previous negativities about not having enough. This also brings a lot of peace within self and in our relationships.

Affirmations don't guarantee the output, instead it guarantees that your frame of mind is positive. We will discuss this point in the next section.

Utilizing the Power of Affirmations

I have been using affirmations for myself and my coachees for a lot of purposes.

Here are some of the example scenarios when affirmations help a lot to keep your mind balanced and you taking the right decision.

Affirmations to Change Belief Systems

We learnt earlier in the chapters, how our belief system works. Based on the beliefs (which might or might not be based on facts), we act, we react, and we design our lives. There are some beliefs that limit us and put us into a fearful or negative mode.

For examples limiting beliefs could be –

1. I can't drive
2. I can't lose weight, no matter how much I try
3. I can't ask for money even if I deserve it
4. I never get complete success, no matter how hard I try

Let's understand this - our beliefs are formed by merely a habitual thinking patterns that we learnt as a child or experienced as an adult.

If these are not working for us in life and limiting us in a big way, counter positive affirmations can help replace these beliefs into more empowered ones.

We have discussed this in detail in previous chapter around Belief system.

Example of counter positive affirmations -

1. I can do anything if I set my mind to it
2. I attract good healthy habits
3. I deserve success and wealth in my life

Affirmations

Affirmations to Combat Fear

There are times in our lives when we start living in the fear the unknown, change or failure.

Here are few very strong affirmations that helped me deal with those fears and instilled a positive belief that things will turn out to be great.

- Whatever happens, happens good for me in the long run
- When the time is right for me, things will happen on it's own
- I'm being saved from something big
- I am giving my best and trust that god/destiny/guiding angel will do whatever is in the best interest of my life
- I am choosing to accept whatever comes my way here on
- This is the opportunity to for me to create a winning story for myself
- There is always a bigger power of universe taking care of us
- Only good things happen to me
- I'm strong enough to bounce back
- I'm surrendering to the universe, to work out what is best for me
- I'm confident, strong, emotionally powerful and resilient
- My good karmas will bring only good for me
- God has graced me with loads of strength and power to help myself and others

Affirmations to Create a Winning Mindset

These affirmations help us to increase our confidence to achieve success and again combat the fear of failure -

- It is easy and simple to achieve success
- Success loves me and always seeks me
- Success is flowing now into my life
- The power of the Universe is helping me to achieve my goals
- Every time I inhale, I fill myself with the energy of prosperity
- I'm a success magnet

Affirmations to Improve Relationships

Affirmations to bring more stability in all kinds of personal and professional relationships -

- People respect and praise me for who I am
- I love everyone around me for their compassion and care for me
- My relationships bring more maturity and peace in my life
- I find like-minded people easily, who provide me with intellectual stimulus
- I feel comfortable and enjoy in social settings
- There is a perfect balance of space and proximity in all my relationships
- I'm able to keep calm and genuinely listen to people
- I gracefully accept people who are different than me
- I am able to share my feelings effortlessly with people who matter to me
- I nurture my relationships with love, genuine care and concern

Affirmations to Improve Self-Esteem & Confidence

- I respect myself for who I am
- I am successful when I put my mind and passion to it
- I continue to learn and grow in all circumstances
- I'm proud of what I've achieved so far in my life
- I choose to standby my decisions as they are sound and reasoned
- I accept the full ownership of my consequences of my decisions
- I can bring change in myself whenever I want to
- I approve of myself and love myself deeply
- My challenges always bring the best out of me
- I have the courage and conviction to take risks and succeed

Affirmations to Forgive and Let – Go

- I choose to forgive myself for my actions and learn my lessons from them
- I choose to start afresh

Affirmations

- I choose to let go
- As I forgive myself, it becomes easier to forgive others
- I choose to be the bigger one and forgive people
- Forgiveness and letting go brings immense peace to me
- I completely release the past and live in the now
- I have a new freedom and a new happiness
- I am grateful to God for my ability to easily forgive
- I am exactly where I am supposed to be right here, right now

The idea of creating affirmations is to change the way we are perceiving a negative emotion, using language.

Affirmations are sometimes blamed to be a process of – fake it till you make it. I don't agree with this. If you fake it, you won't ever be able to make it in case of affirmations and visualizations.

> **"One needs to be in complete sync when writing or reading affirmations."**

Complete sync means, when you are writing an affirmation – "I'm peaceful and happy" – you are not only utilizing your body to **write this down** and **see & read this affirmation**, but also **feeling it inside** to be true.

Unless you feel how it feels to be peaceful and happy, it won't become a truth or a belief for you.

At-least when you are writing or reading an affirmation, you have to completely believe and visualize how it would feel if what you are writing was true. The more you do that, the faster you will realize the change within you.

> **"Our brain is very innocent. It doesn't differentiate between reality and imagination. If you imagine or internalize something to be true, your brain will start functioning accordingly."**

When and How to Repeat Affirmations

1. Devote some special times during the day for repeating them
2. Repeat them wherever you are, and whenever you want and have the time
3. Keep them handy and visible whenever you want them

Before starting, ask yourself whether you **really** want to get what you want to affirm for. If you have doubts and are not really sure that you want it, your doubts will stand in your way. This is one of the reasons why people do not get results, and then lose their belief in this power.

You need to deal with these doubts and fears first, hence create affirmations for these fears too, alongwith the ones for main subject.

In the next few pages, I'm sharing a collection of affirmations for different dimensions of life. Hope you like them and choose the ones that resonate with you the most and start practicing!

Career

1. I love my career as it gives me complete job satisfaction.
2. I love my career as it allows me to grow as well as makes me financially abundant.
3. I am able to balance my career with my family life so that both are in harmony.
4. My job offers me great career prospects, opportunities & monetary compensation.
5. I am a valued person at my workplace and my voice is always heard respectfully.
6. I am happy that the work I do benefits me as well as the society I live in.
7. I always attract the best projects because of my positive mental attitude.
8. I am ever enthusiastic and my enthusiasm rubs off on my co-workers and this results in a great work day for all of us.
9. I am a born entrepreneur. I recognize and seize opportunities as and when they appear.
10. I am a master salesman. My customers love and trust me and my order book is overflowing with orders.

Affirmations

11. My work ethic ensures that I get regular promotions and monetary incentives.
12. Self discipline is my forte. At the workplace, work is my priority and at home, family is my priority.
13. I take full responsibility for my work. 'The buck stops here' is my motto.
14. I follow the rule 'Work is Worship.' Diligence in work, honesty in attitude and a positive frame of mind open up new horizons for me.
15. I take good care of my juniors and guide them appropriately. I am friendly with my colleagues and respectful to my seniors.
16. Career to me is a means to an end. That end is happiness and fulfillment of potential and my career is providing it to me in abundance.
17. I am doing my best in my career and giving my everything without reservation. The fruits of my labour are always so sweet.
18. My main aim is satisfaction of my customers and I strive my best to achieve that aim.
19. I am manifesting my dream job.
20. I am always open to new opportunities to find my dream job.
21. I am highly confident in myself and in my abilities to perform my dream job.
22. I am worthy of doing a job that I love.
23. I clear my dream job interview easily and effortlessly.
24. I am attracting a positive job environment.
25. I am working happily and positively with everyone at my dream job.
26. Every career move that I make turns out to be a magical experience.
27. I am a career magnet – I am attracting excellent job prospects all the time.
28. I am being paid very well to do an exciting and rewarding job.
29. I am now attracting the perfect career for my talents.
30. I am so happy and grateful for the new Dream Job that I have found.
31. I have all the knowledge and skills to perform at my Dream Job.
32. I have a magical vibration to work happily in my dream job.
33. I am attracting only positive outcome at my new job.

34. I find it easy to network with others.
35. The Universe is making all the perfect arrangement for my dream job.
36. My ideal employment is coming to me right now.
37. I deserve to work in a dream job.
38. I have found my dream job.
39. I am well-paid and having a rewarding job.
40. I am happy to work with a good boss and great team-mates.
41. Everyone around me is helping me to go from success to success at my dream job.

Finance

1. I am a magnet for money. Prosperity is drawn to me
2. Money comes to me in expected and unexpected ways
3. I move from poverty thinking to abundance thinking
4. I am worthy of making more money
5. I am open and receptive to all the wealth life offers me
6. I embrace new avenues of income
7. I welcome an unlimited source of income and wealth in my life
8. I release all negative energy over money
9. Money comes to me easily and effortlessly
10. I use money to better my life and the lives of others
11. Wealth constantly flows into my life
12. My actions create constant prosperity
13. I am aligned with the energy of abundance
14. I constantly attract opportunities that create more money
15. My finances improve beyond my dreams
16. Money is the root of joy and comfort
17. Money and spirituality can co-exist in harmony
18. Money and love can be friends

Affirmations

19. I am the master of my wealth
20. I am able to handle large sums of money
21. I am at peace with having a lot of money
22. I can handle massive success with grace
23. Money expands my life's opportunities and experiences
24. Money creates positive impact in my life
25. I am wealthy
26. I always have money
27. I attract financial abundance
28. My mind is finely tuned for attracting massive wealth
29. I always think positively about money
30. I have many financial opportunities
31. I always find a way to make a large profit
32. I am rich and prosperous
33. My life is full of abundance
34. I am focused on achieving wealth
35. Money flows effortlessly into my life
36. Financial abundance is my birthright
37. I am a magnet for money
38. I am receiving money every day
39. Money comes easily and frequently
40. Money flows to me from multiple sources
41. I'm wealthy
42. I'm financially free
43. Save, invest and reinvest is my mantra for financial success.
44. I have a very healthy relationship with money. I treat money with respect and handle it with confidence
45. The prices of the shares in which I have invested are always growing

Personal Growth

1. Every-day, in every way, I am getting better and better
2. Every failure can be a learning experience
3. I live in the present moment
4. I create value in other peoples' lives
5. I am always changing
6. I am worthy of positive relationships in my life
7. I wish the best for everyone
8. I learn something new every-day
9. I am genuinely interested in other people's well being
10. I have many strengths
11. I concentrate on things that I can influence or control
12. Listening to my emotions can help guide me to make better decisions
13. My anxiety is motivation to change or improve
14. I can overcome obstacles in my life
15. I am a positive role model to others
16. I will try something different today
17. Stepping outside of my comfort zone is necessary for growth
18. People are generally good
19. I forgive easily
20. I have a wealthy and supportive social circle
21. What doesn't kill me only makes me stronger
22. My past is one big learning experience
23. I must be the change I wish to see in the world
24. I am understanding of others
25. This too shall pass
26. I can find happiness in every moment
27. I'm a proactive problem-solver

Affirmations

28. When I open my mind and senses, I'm much more creative
29. I can create my own positive energy
30. When people get to know me, they really like me
31. I'm great at creating and executing successful plans
32. I can see the bigger picture
33. I see money as a useful tool for helping myself and others
34. I take small steps everyday to be more healthy
35. I'm dedicated to my passion in life
36. I have the resources to take care of my family
37. I determine the meaning of my life
38. Every decision I make helps shape my destiny even more beautifully
39. Whenever I take risks, I reap big rewards
40. I remain focused on what matters
41. I participate in life
42. I can think rationally and intelligently whenever required
43. I'm dedicated to self-improvement
44. I treat others with kindness and respect
45. I love and accept my body
46. When I love myself, I allow others to love me too
47. Today, I open my mind to the endless opportunities surrounding me

Health

1. Every day in every way I am getting healthier and healthier and feeling better and better
2. I eat healthy, nutritious food that benefits my body and drink a large quantity of water that cleanses my body
3. I love myself and I am perfectly healthy
4. Every cell in my body is health conscious. I am a health freak.
5. Every passing day my body becomes more energetic, more healthy

6. I treat my body as a temple. It is holy, it is clean, and it is full of goodness
7. I breathe deeply, exercise regularly and feed only good nutritious food to my body
8. I am free of all life-threatening diseases
9. I express my deep gratitude to God and everybody in my life
10. Healthy, wealthy and wise is my motto. My body is healthy, I am wealthy, and my mind is wise
11. I am ready to enjoy perfect health
12. I am capable and prepared to heal my body
13. An endless supply of healing energy streams through me at all times
14. I deserve to live a healthy life
15. I attract pure health and wholeness every day
16. I love exercising and eating healthy foods
17. I am getting better with every passing moment
18. I am grateful for the healing that is happening in my body.
19. I take care of my body with respect and love
20. I give myself permission to have perfect health
21. My body deserves to be whole
22. I am known for my positive energy and healthy lifestyle
23. I always choose options that are best for my health
24. I love taking care of myself
25. I manifest perfect health by making smart choices
26. I produce miraculous results by living a healthy lifestyle
27. I enjoy being healthy, happy and whole
28. I am surrounded by people who encourage me to be healthy
29. People admire my healthy lifestyle choices
30. I admire other healthy people and I'm inspired to learn from them
31. My lifestyle choices inspire and motivate people
32. My perfect health is necessary

33. I am a beneficial presence on this planet
34. I listen to the messages my body sends me
35. I respond to my body's messages with patience and understanding
36. I create the exact lifestyle I want to have with enthusiasm
37. I choose happiness and health in my life
38. I celebrate life every day
39. Miracles and magic surround me everywhere I go
40. I am healthy and whole
41. My body is being healed right now.

Family

1. Every day I thank god for my wonderful family
2. Every person in my family is healthy and happy
3. I allow great experiences to enrich my children's lives
4. I allow my children the freedom to be themselves
5. I always respond to my spouse (name) and children with patience and love
6. I always treat my spouse and children with love and understanding
7. My actions, thoughts and words inspire my children to be role models
8. I am setting a great example for my children
9. I maintain peace and calm when speaking to members of my family
10. I am immensely proud of my children
11. I am providing my children with a brilliant future
12. My family is in support of my ambitions and goals
13. I enjoy that I am raising children who are happy and optimistic
14. There is peace and harmony in my family
15. My confidence and optimism brings out the best in my children and partner
16. My partner and I are always in agreement about what is best for our children
17. I am loved and respected by my spouse and children
18. I am communicating honestly and lovingly with my spouse and children every moment

19. I focus on love in my family
20. I enjoy spending time with my spouse and children
21. I am in love with the feeling of being with child
22. I love that my children are becoming more independent
23. I instill empowering beliefs to my children
24. I am always listening intently to my spouse and children when they speak
25. I am loved and accepted by my parents for who I AM and all that I AM
26. I am grateful for the experiences and lessons that I have learned in my family
27. I am considerate of the feelings of my family
28. My siblings and I are always close and supportive of each other
29. I inculcate values and discipline in my children in a loving way
30. I encourage and bless all the talents that my children have
31. I have a home that is full of joy and peace
32. I have confidence in the strengths and coping abilities of my children
33. I am loved by my parents unconditionally
34. I choose this day to enjoy the life and presence of my children
35. It is okay to hold beliefs that are different from my parents
36. My love for my children helps them to refrain from peer pressure
37. My family is a source of continued joy
38. I'm continually becoming closer to my mom
39. I'm continually becoming closer to my dad
40. My kind words help to bring the family together
41. I'm able to afford classes for my children
42. My children always return safely to me
43. My family and I always remain safe
44. My family friends and I are all receiving abundance now
45. Being adopted is part of my path

Affirmations

46. My children and spouse trust me to come and openly share
47. I open my ears and my heart, listening for the truth behind the words

Relationships

1. I have nothing but love for all
2. I love everyone and in turn everyone loves me
3. I give and receive love freely and joyfully
4. I find love everywhere I go. Life is amazing!
5. I love being with people who bring out the best in me
6. I see myself as being filled with love and happiness
7. I feel like I matter. I am a contribution to this world
8. I accept that I don't have to do anything to be loved and happy
9. I love myself totally
10. I accept that I can receive love and happiness right now!
11. I accept that I am infinitely loved
12. I attract relationships to me that are for the highest good of all
13. I love sharing amazing conversations with my friends, family and lover
14. I enjoy and thrive in the company of great friends
15. I love laughing and having fun in my relationships
16. I love that my relationships are in harmony with my highest good
17. I accept that I am loved and treasured for who I really AM
18. I give and receive love freely and fully in all my relationships
19. I love being supported by my friends, family, and relationships
20. I enjoy sharing the real me in relationships
21. I know with every fiber of my being that the Universe is bringing me only the most supportive, loving, and awesome relationships!
22. My relationships of the past, present and future are now enfolded in love and harmonized for the good of all
23. Everyone in my life is supportive of me

24. I see God's love in action in all my relationships and difficulties are wonderful opportunities for me to have a change of heart
25. As I change my heart in relationships, my life becomes wonderful
26. Every person I encounter has an important message for me
27. I attracted the perfect companion
28. With innocent perception, I bring God to bear in my life. All is possible with the power of love
29. As I see the face of God in others, all my encounters are elevated to greater meaning and inspired outcomes.
30. I bless all my relationships with forgiveness and acceptance
31. I easily and purposefully engage the energies I need to give to others according to what I want to experience from them
32. I release and let go, in order to recognize my power at shaping my life
33. I uplift and inspire everyone around me

Social Life

1. I am confident when in social situations
2. My social skills are extra ordinary, people love me for my social skills
3. I can speak confidently to anyone
4. I enjoy speaking to new people
5. I have naturally good social skills
6. I always speak clearly
7. I am able to deal with anything that anybody says to me
8. I always stand up for myself
9. I am relaxed when I speak to new people
10. I am outgoing
11. I uplift and inspire everyone around me
12. I am comfortable in groups
13. I am comfortable in social situations
14. I am smart and witty, everybody loves me

Affirmations

15. I have a lot to offer the world
16. I remain calm and confident in groups
17. It is safe and comfortable for me to interact with people
18. I feel safe in social environments
19. I welcome new social situations into my life today
20. I love meeting new people!
21. I am a beautiful person and have a lot to offer the world!
22. I love making small talk!
23. I have a lot of interesting things to say!
24. I love being among other people
25. It is safe and comfortable for me to socialize
26. Other people love me!
27. I easily release what other people think of me
28. I always love and approve of myself!
29. I always have interesting things to say!
30. My inner beauty radiates from me!
31. I make conversation with others easily
32. People love and accept me the way I am
33. I'm able to be myself in social situations
34. People love talking to me and show genuine interest in what I do
35. I exude positivity and confidence in social situations
36. I accept the differences and love to observe and admire them in social situations
37. People get attracted with my genuine approach to things and non-judgmental nature

Attitude

1. All days are great days in my life!
2. Each new day brings more joy into my life!

3. Every day I experience how magnificent life can be
4. Every day in my life is better than the day before
5. Every day is a perfect day for me
6. Everything is super in my life
7. I alone control my attitude
8. I always see the bright side in life
9. I am a high achiever with big dreams
10. I am a manifestation of my beliefs about myself, therefore I believe that I am terrific!
11. I am a radiant being and enjoy life to its fullest
12. I am a winner!
13. I am ambition personified
14. I am excited to be here!
15. I am high on life!
16. I am in a fantastic mood today!
17. I am in complete control of my life.
18. I am in it to win it!
19. I am in my power place wherever I am.
20. I am irresistible!
21. I am large and in charge!
22. I am outstanding!
23. I am passionate about life!
24. I am remarkable!
25. I am the embodiment of perfection
26. I am the king of my world!
27. I am the queen of my world!
28. I am in control of my own thinking
29. I think only thoughts that create and fulfill the best in me

Affirmations

30. My mind is constantly in tune with the positive
31. I am full of great thoughts and positive ideas
32. My thoughts are bright, cheerful and enthusiastic
33. I consciously choose what I think, that is beneficial to me

Create Your Own Affirmations

While there are thousands of affirmations available in the cloud, and quite a few in this book, it is always advisable to create them for yourself.

Simple affirmations that you resonate with the most are the key to make it work.

Also, at times one needs very specific affirmations, at that time, it is important that you know what the rules are, to create those.

Let me give you an example of how these affirmations really helped me stay positive in my low times.

I was trying to conceive from 6 years after our marriage, tried almost everything possible. Finally, we went to a specialist who advised to go for IVF. IVF is a painful process, however, I was ready to go to any extent of pain to have a baby.

Finally, after the procedures were complete, I had to wait for the results. I was very nervous and filled up with all kinds of fears. This is when Snehal taught me to use affirmations. All my nervousness vanished, and I can't thank her enough, for that was one of the toughest waiting time for me in life.

Here are the rules that I learnt in the initial days and follow them to get maximum results even till date -

- Write what you "Want" instead of what you don't want

  My pregnancy reports are positive

  Everyone around me is thrilled with the news

- Affirmations cannot have any negative word

  Instead of writing "*There is no complication in my pregnancy*," write "*My pregnancy is completely smooth and healthy*"

- Best affirmations are written in present tense

  I'm pregnant instead of I'll be pregnant

- ✓ Make them personal, use "I" so it is easier for your brain to believe in it
- ✓ Closing of your affirmations can be best done with the following statements –

    a. I choose to create all of this or something better

    b. I trust whatever happens in my life will be only for my good

    c. "I will respect and accept whatever happens with full faith and hope for betterment"

Summary | Chapter 16

- Affirmations are sentences aimed to affect the conscious and the subconscious mind

- The words composing the affirmation, automatically and involuntarily, bring up related mental images into the mind, which could inspire, energize and motivate

- Repeating affirmations, and the resultant mental images, affect the subconscious mind, which in turn, influences the behavior, habits, actions and reactions

- Affirm with love, faith, feeling and interest, and feel and believe that your desire has already been fulfilled. This kind of thinking will accelerate its fulfillment.

Reader Reflections

- Are you living with any fear? If yes, then convert those fears into affirmations and write them down with full conviction. Feel how it will feel if your affirmation comes true.

  Example: If you have a fear that you will fail an exam, write an affirmation: "I've got awesome grades in my exams and everyone around me is congratulating me"

17

Winning Frames

In the world of NLP (Neuro-Linguistic Programming), mental frames provide context and focus on what we want to achieve.

Have you ever caught yourself saying anything like this?

"I wish this happened differently"

"Why did this happen to me"

"What's the cause of my unhappiness/loneliness"

This is a very natural way of our brain to react. Our brain loves to put us into a victim zone, because there we feel very safe. However, with that safety comes the stress, negativity and helplessness.

On the other hand, if we are able to re-program ourselves to look at the present and future, it can tremendously change the feelings.

Example:

"What can I do about this now"

"What resources do I have to make it better next time"

Thinking from this frame of reference brings the feelings of empowerment, positively and hope in us.

For the same situation, only changing the frame of mind or the questions that we ask ourselves, can bring a whole lot of difference and make us win in the long run.

I'm putting together a list of questions that can help you experience different frames of mind. Nothing is bad or good, all these frames can be utilized in different contexts in order to win.

Calibrate how you are feeling while answering these questions, and then reflect on where you can utilize this frame better.

Types of Frames

1. Blame Frame

Blame frame is problem oriented and lead to experiences of limitation and lack of choice. They demand explanations of why you don't have what you want, excuses and justifications.

- What's wrong?
- Why do I have this problem? "How long have I had this problem?"
- How does this limit me?
- What does this program stop me from doing what I want to do?
- Whose fault is it that I have the problem?
- When was the last time I experienced this problem?

2. Outcome Frame

Outcome frame is towards the future and towards resources, and usually leaves people feeling hopeful and capable. It provides focus on what you want to achieve, the ensuing effects and resources required to achieve it.

- What do I want?
- When do I want it?
- How will I know that I have it?
- When I get what I want, what else in my life will improve?
- What resources do I have available to help me with this?
- How can I best utilize the resources that I have?
- What are the external resources that I need?
- What am I going to begin doing now to get what I want?

As blame frame occurs to us by default, it is only through conscious efforts that we can program ourselves to think from outcome frame of reference.

Blame frame is often used to catch attention, for example in an advertisement. You can catch some raw nerves very effectively using blame frame. However, ensure that you spend more time on outcome frame.

Here are some more frames of reference, helpful in different situations.

3. Ecology Frame

A person, who pursues his outcome without regard for the impact on other systems (e.g., body systems, family, work environment, community), has not taken into account the ecology frame.

For example, going on a diet may result in a good-looking body, but is the diet good for your immune system?

For an outcome that you have at work, what is the effect on your co-workers and can you mitigate any negative effects?

Is your outcome congruent with other outcomes that you have or plan to set?

4. Evidence Frame

The evidence frame is used as a gauge to assess how well you are progressing towards your outcome and to know when your outcome has been achieved. As a result, you will know if corrective action should be taken or if a new or modified outcome should be set. Simply, how will you know when you have achieved your outcome? What will you see, hear, feel or experience?

5. As if Frame

This frame has many applications and is based on acting 'as if' a desired state or outcome has been achieved or 'as if' someone else is giving you information:

- For an outcome, act as if you have already achieved your outcome. Live your dreams now and allow reality to catch up!
- When negotiating or problem solving, you can explore other possibilities by saying, "Let's proceed as if I agree to this demand or take your proposed course of action. What would you do for me, or what would happen as a result?"
- If a key person is missing from a meeting, you may say, "Let's act as if Sue is present. What would she suggest?"
- For project planning, you may wish act as if the project has been successfully completed and then ask what steps were necessary to reach this outcome. This approach may highlight some important information that is not obvious when planning from the present.

6. Backtrack Frame

This frame can be used to check agreement and understanding during and at the conclusion of a meeting, to update a new arrival or to restart a discussion.

Backtracking is accompanied by reviewing the available information using the keywords and tonality of those who brought the information forward.

We all filter information differently and may come to significantly different conclusions. Backtracking is a way to ensure everyone has the same understanding of what was discussed and decided and helps to maintain a course towards the desired outcome.

The winning idea is to make it a habit to look at important things with different frames of mind. That helps people take right decisions, and even understand other people's point of view.

Another important type of framing, that impacts how we deal with challenges is called "Re-framing." Reframing helps us a lot to feel better about a situation.

Reframing

It's a natural process that we all go through in terms of how we seek to make sense of the world. We attribute meaning to everything that we encounter and every experience that we have.

In life, nothing is intrinsically good or bad, positive or negative. Events or experiences don't, of themselves, have any meaning whatsoever, they have only the meaning we give to them. That meaning is determined to a large degree by the frame in which we perceive it. When the frame changes so does the meaning, and our response to it – the way we feel and how we act.

In NLP, this is called reframing, an important technique you can use with yourself and with others to free them from the shackles of rigid thinking and to therefore have more choices.

At its simplest, reframing involves seeing things from a different perspective, in another light, from an alternative point of view.

Some common examples of reframing are given below for you understand it better –

Example	Reframing
I really doubt that I can do anything about this	What is one small step that you might take?
I don't want to work on that now because it makes me feel sad	What small part of that might you work on for now, that might even leave you feeling a bit more happy?
I feel stressed that my husband keeps demanding more and more of my time, while I want to spend more time to pursue my passion	Have you considered the fact that your husband loves you so much that instead of going out or having an affair, he wants to work it out with you.
That always happen to me	Sometimes we even do that to ourselves. Perhaps it'd be useful to explore if you're somehow doing that to yourself too.
My parents are very demanding and controlling, I just can't stand them, neither can I leave them	Well, at-least they are alive and active enough to take care of you.

Two most common questions that help reframe almost all the challenges –

1. What else this could mean?
2. In what way could this be positive or a resource?

One thing that's important to understand is that reframing isn't about taking a rose-tinted view that everything is wonderful.

The aim of reframing is to achieve a more realistic perspective on reality. Reframes have to make at least as much sense to people as the way they thought about things before, and they have to match their view of reality.

Summary | Chapter 17

Frames are nothing but the different angles in which we can see the same situation.

Everyone has some default frame that is set for most of the challenges. Example – there are some people who will by default blame others for the difficult situations they are in, while there are others who by default look at what can do about the situation instead of brooding over it.

No frame is right or wrong, it's just that once we understand what different frames are, it becomes easier to choose which frame we want to look at things from.

Here are different frames that were discussed in the chapter

1. **Blame frame:** Commonly used to gain attention, sympathy, evoke negative feelings. Works well in advertisement world, root cause analysis to avoid a challenge in future proactively etc. Focused on digging the past.

2. **Outcome frame:** A winning frame to get out of a challenging situation and feel positive and empowered. Focused on looking at the future.

3. **Ecology frame:** This frame helps look at all the aspects and create equilibrium in your life. Primarily used for goal setting, current situation analysis.

4. **Evidence Frame:** This frame is primarily used to visualize the success in details and determine the criterion. Used in case you need to determine the effectiveness of your actions, or measure the return on your investment of money, efforts and time.

5. **As-if frame:** This frame is very useful when one is not able to visualize an outcome or to think beyond fears and current beliefs. If you feel stuck in a conversation, as-if frame helps you to move ahead with more possibilities.

6. **Backtrack frame:** This frame helps you look back, review what was agreed or not agreed, set the objectives for future, get on the same page with others.

Another concept shared in this chapter is that of "Reframing."

Reframing is used to help understand the same challenge in different and more positive perspective.

18
Empowering Beliefs for Winning Mindset

Hope you enjoyed reading the book and have already set your mind to bring a massive change in your life.

By now you must have realized the power of the WINNING mindset, and how we can re-program our mind to success.

For your quick reference, I'm putting together a list of beliefs that made people mega successful in life in various facets.

In case, you face any self-doubt or contradiction with your existing beliefs, just put the "AS IF" frame. Visualize, as if you had this belief – how would you feel. Break the limiting pattern of your beliefs

Empowering Beliefs for Daily Practice

1. I believe in the power of NOW, and make the most of it
2. I am deeply aware of my surroundings and self, due to which I build fruitful relationships and make winning decisions
3. I have full confidence on my abilities which always land me to the right place at the right time
4. I always get adequate resources when I need them, so I don't bother about "how" – I know if I set my mind to it, I'll get it

Empowering Beliefs for Winning Mindset

5. When I do things right with the right intention, I always get amazing results
6. I always get way more than what I expect
7. I know that if things aren't working out, something better is in store for me. I trust my destiny/god and guardian angels
8. I am always protected by the divine powers
9. My sub-conscious guides me through, whenever I am in dilemma or feel stuck
10. I attract most of the people in my life, who understand my intentions and love to work with me
11. I am able to dissociate from a challenge and look at it from different angles
12. I have an innate power to manage my emotions when I really want to
13. At any point in time, I can always gather back myself and bounce back.
14. I am grounded and that quality helps me deeply connect with people
15. I have the ability to come up with unique ideas and bring thought leadership
16. I have the ability to accept and adapt change quicker than anyone

Summing Up

If you learnt even 1% of what's written in the book, then do share your learning with at-least 5 more people.

This famous star fish thrower story sums up my intention.

One day a man was walking along the beach, when he noticed a boy hurriedly picking up and gently throwing back star fish into the ocean.

Approaching the boy, he asked, "Young man, what are you doing?"

The boy replied, "Throwing starfish back into the ocean. The surf is up and the tide is going out. If I don't throw them back, they'll die."

The man laughed to himself and said, "Don't you realize there are miles and miles of beach and hundreds of starfish? You can't make any difference!"

After listening politely, the boy bent down, picked up another starfish, and threw it into the surf. Then, smiling at the man, he said – **"I made a difference to that one."**
– **by Loren Eiseley**.

References

- 7 habits of highly effective people: *Stephen Covey*
- You can heal your life: *Louis Hay*
- Emotional Intelligence: *Daniel Goleman*
- Neuro-Linguistic Programming: *Joseph o' Connor*
- Awaken the Giant within you: *Tony Robbins*
- The Secret: *Rhonda Byrne*
- The Power of Now: *by Swami Vivekananda*
- Happiness is your creation: *by Swami Rama*
- The art of joyful living: *by Swami Rama*
- The fearless living: *by Swami Rama*
- Bhagwad-Gita As it is: *A C Bhaktivedanta & Swami Prabhupada*
- The Alchemist: *Paula Coelho*
- Who Moved my Cheese: Dr. Spencer Johnson
- Blog: Coaching and Action Learning: Basic Guidelines to Reframing — to Seeing Things Differently, *By Carter McNamara on February 2, 2012*
- Benefits of Gratitude: *Happierhuman.com*
- 5 Tips to Supercharge Your Gratitude List and Infuse Your Life With Joy, *By Tree Franklyn*

NeuCode Talent Academy LLP

Head-office: Bangalore, India

Phone: +91 9731601397

E-mail: info@neucodetalent.com

Website: www.neucodetalent.com

FB: https://www.facebook.com/NeuCodeTalent/

NeuCode Talent Academy is an organization founded by the author, that aims to build more emotional resilience and awareness in people. Feel free to reach out to us, for any queries, comments, coaching or details.